Texas Local History

A Source Book for Available Town and County Histories, Local Memoirs and Genealogical Records

1983 Edition

Compiled by

Tom Munnerlyn

EAKIN PRESS AUSTIN, TEXAS

FIRST EDITION

Published in the United States of America
By Eakin Press, P.O. Box 23066, Austin, Texas 78735

ISBN 0-89015-378-7

TABLE OF CONTENTS

PREFACE

This Source Book

The present book was developed to bring together in one volume a listing of all the materials on Texas local history that are currently available for sale. The majority of the books in the local history classification are published by individuals or local history and genealogy organizations rather than by dedicated book publishers. Most of these type publications are produced in limited quantity and distributed on a local basis. In some cases, the books are sold on a prepayment subscription basis to support the cost of publication which means that the book is virtually "sold-out" before it gets printed.

Entries were gathered from publishers catalogs, advertisements, book reviews, and through correspondence with publishers, authors, librarians, historical organzations, genealogy groups and chambers of commerce throughout the state. Their responses are very much appreciated. Even though there are over a thousand items listed in this book, there are probably several hundred more items that exist but were missed during the past year of searching.

Books included are considered to be historical in content and identified with a particular county or counties in Texas. Fiction,poetry, geology and archeology publications are excluded. Although some of the books are classified as being out-of-print from the original publisher, they were included if a source was located having sufficient copies to fill multiple orders. Also, the source shown for a particular book may or may not be the original publisher.

The county descriptions in this book were prepared by my friend Henry Ingram. These entries were designed for the reader to be able to quickly refer to the histories of the county or counties from which a particular county was derived and also to look to adjoining county histories for additional information on a particular area.

The Next Source Book

It is planned to publish the next source book in early 1984. It is hoped that the subsequent edition will be larger in content with entries for all 254 Texas counties. Perhaps the gaps that exist in the county listings of the present book will inspire some historian to begin working on a new history of their community or county.

An author, organization or publisher may have their publication included at no charge. All that is needed is to send complete bibliographic details to the compiler at the address shown at the bottom of the next page. Bibliographic details that are needed: title, subtitle, author, place of publication, date of publication, number of pages, whether or not the book is illustrated, contains a bibliography or index; size of the book in inches, whether paper or hardcover binding, price and address to order. A brief description of the contents is also desired.

Any additions, corrections and deletions to any entries in the present source book are also requested.

How to Order from this Book

Section one contains a listing of histories, records and periodicals under each county heading. Section two contains basic state and regional books and periodicals that will be useful for research on people, places and events in Texas history.

Immediately after the price that is shown for each publication will be a name or group of letters which denotes the source for the publication. Refer to that name or group of letters in section three to find the address to write to obtain the particular publication.

The price that is shown with each entry **does not include state sales tax or shipping costs. Prices are also subject to change,** usually upward! There are two ways to order: (1) Write or telephone before sending any money, so as to verify the availability, price and shipping charges for the book. This is the recommended method. (2) The least preferred is to send a check or money order for the price shown plus 5% tax, if applicable, plus an estimated amount for shipping. In either method, **enclose a self-addressed stamped envelope** with your order to speed a reply or the return of your money should the material no longer be available.

If a source has exhausted their supply of an item, refer to the last section for information on ordering **out-of-print** books.

Abbreviations Used

biblio. - bibliography
ed. - edition
folio - Size, over 13 inches tall
ill. - illustrated
p. - pages
pc. - papercover
un. - unnumbered
vol. - volume
4to - Size, from 11 to 13 inches tall

Tom Munnerlyn
2202 Colgate Lane
Austin, Tx 78723

SECTION 1 - TOWN AND COUNTY PUBLICATIONS

ANDERSON

Created from Houston County, organized in 1846, named for K.L. Anderson, last vice-president of the Republic of Texas. County seat Palestine; other towns are Franston and Elkhart. Bordering counties are Henderson, Freestone, Leon, Houston and Cherokee.

ANDERSON COUNTY CENSUS RECORDS 1850. $14.00. Heritage.

ANDERSON COUNTY LAND TITLES. Compiled by F. T. Ingmire. $6.95. Ingmire.

ANDERSON COUNTY, TEXAS MARRIAGE RECORDS 1846-1869. Compiled by Russell. pc. $6.00. Ingmire.

CENTENNIAL NOTEBOOK. A Collage of Reminiscence. By Carl Avera. Palestine,Tx, 1976, 46p.,pc. 4to. $2.25. Palestine.

ANDREWS

Created 1876 from Bexar County, organized 1910, named for Richard Andrews. County seat Andrews; other towns include Florey and Frankel City. Bounded by Gaines, Dawson, Martin, Midland, Ector and Winkler Counties, and by New Mexico on the west.

ORIGINAL GRANTEE, PATENTEE. ARCHER/ANDREWS COUNTY. Compiled by F.T. Ingmire. St. Louis, 1979, 29p.,index, 4to. $6.95. Ingmire.

ANGELINA

Created and organized in 1846 from Nacogdoches County, named for Angelina River. County seat is Lufkin; other towns include Diboll, Huntington, Zavalla, and Herty. Bounded by Cherokee, Nacogdoches, San Augustine, Jasper, Tyler, Polk, Trinity and Houston Counties.

ANGELINA COUNTY CEMETERY RECORDS. Vol. 2. January 1969 through August 1981. $12.50. LGHS.

ANGELINA COUNTY CENSUS RECORDS 1850. $6.00. Heritage.

ANGELINA COUNTY MARRIAGE RECORDS 1846-1897. Compiled by Mrs. L. S. Krisch. $11.95. Ingmire.

ANGELINA COUNTY, TEXAS 1850 CENSUS AND FIRST TAX PAPERS. Compiled by Mrs. L. S. Krisch. $7.95. Ingmire.

HISTORY AND DESCRIPTION OF ANGELINA COUNTY, TEXAS by A.W. Haltom. Austin, 1969. Reprint of 1888 ed., 98p. $7.50. Ranger.

LAND OF THE LITTLE ANGEL. A History of Angelina County. Edited by Bob Bowman. Lufkin, 1976. 353p.,ill., biblio.,index, 4to. $34.95. Lufkin.

THE LUFKIN THAT WAS. The Centennial Photo-Album of Lufkin. Edited by Bob Bowman. Lufkin. $34.95. Lufkin.

ORIGINAL GRANTEE, PATENTEE. Pt.1 Angelina County Land Titles. Pt. 2 Aransas County Land Titles. Compiled by F.T. Ingmire. St. Louis, 1979. 34p.,4to.,$6.95. Ingmire.

TEXAS CENSUS 1850. Vol. 12. Compiled by V. K. Carpenter. 1979. Reprint ed. pc. $10.00. Presley.

ARANSAS

Created and organized 1871 from Refugio County, named for Rio Nuestra Senora del Aranzazu. County seat Rockport; other towns include Aransas Pass, Fulton and Lamar. Bounded by San Patricio, Refugio, and Calhoun Counties and the Gulf of Mexico.

ARANSAS PASS, TEXAS. By Harriett Johnson, et al. Aransas Pass, Tx, 1976. 321p., ill., pc. $5.00. Ranger.

ORIGINAL GRANTEE, PATENTEE. Part 1 Angelina County Land Titles. Part 2 Aransas County Land Titles. Compiled by F.T. Ingmire. St. Louis, 1979. 34p., 4to. $6.95. Ingmire.

TEXAS COASTAL BEND. People and Places. By Alpha K. Wood. 1979. 2d Ed. $10.00. Rockport.

ARCHER

Created from Fannin Land District 1858, organized 1880, named for Dr. Branch T. Archer. County seat Archer City; other towns include Windthorst, Scotland, Megargel, and Holliday. Bounded by Wichita, Clay, Jack, Young, Baylor, Wilbarger and Throckmorton Counties.

ARCHER COUNTY CENTENNIAL PICTURE BOOK. $4.00. Archer.

ARCHER COUNTY FAMILY HISTORY. Paper $4, Cloth $10.Archer.

ARCHER COUNTY PIONEERS. A History of Archer County, Texas By Ruth Jones O'Keefe. Hereford, Tx., 1969. 133p., ill.,index, 4to. $10.00. Ranger.

ARCHER COUNTY TEXAS CEMETERIES. Compiled by Mr. & Mrs. O.V. Hampton, 1970, 87p.,pc. $12.50. TSGS.

ORIGINAL GRANTEE PATENTEE. Archer County/Andrews County. Compiled by F.T. Ingmire. St. Louis, 1979. 29p., 4to. $6.95.Ingmire.

TRAILS THROUGH ARCHER. A Centennial History 1880-1980. By Jack Loftin. Burnet, 1979. 577p.,ill.,biblio.,index. $18.50. Ranger.

ARMSTRONG

Created 1876 from Bexar County, organized 1890, named for a pioneer family. County seat Claude; other towns include Washburn, Wayside and Goodnight. Bounded by Randall, Potter, Gray, Donley, Briscoe and Swisher Counties.

ORIGINAL GRANTEE, PATENTEE. Armstrong County, Texas Land Titles, Bastrop County, Texas Land Titles. Compiled by F.T. Ingmire. St. Louis, 1979. 30p., index, 4to. pc. $6.95. Ingmire.

ATASCOSA

Created and organized from Bexar County in 1856. The name means "boggy" in Spanish. County seat Pleasanton; other towns include Poteet, Lytle, Campbellton, Christine, Jourdanton and Charlotte. Bounded by Bexar,Medina,Frio,LaSalle,McMullen,Live Oak,Karnes and Wilson Counties.

A COLORED PICTURE BROCHURE. By Centennial Committee-Lytle Chamber of Commerce. 1982. pc. $3.00. Lytle.

PATCHWORK. A History of Lytle. A Bicentennial Project of the Lytle Womans Club. 1976. $10.00. Wanjura.

A VAQUERO OF THE BRUSH COUNTRY. By J.Frank Dobie. Austin, 1929. Reprint ed. 1981. 302p.,ill., index, pc. $7.95. Ranger.

AUSTIN

Selected by Stephen F. Austin for his colony, created in 1836 and organized in 1837. County seat Bellville; other towns include Sealy, San Felipe, Wallis, New Ulm and Industry. Bounded by Washington, Waller, Fort Bend, Wharton, Colorado and Fayette Counties.

AUSTIN COUNTY CENSUS RECORDS 1850. $14.50. Heritage.

AUSTIN COUNTY, TEXAS MINUTES OF BOARD OF COMMISSIONERS. Compiled by G. White. Austin, 1972. 150p., 4to.,pc.$12.50.Ingmire.

CROSSROADS AT SAN FELIPE. By Noel Grisham. Burnet, Tx. 96p., ill.,index, pc. $12.50. Ingmire.

FIRST SETTLERS OF AUSTIN COUNTY, TEXAS. Edited by G. White, index, pc. $12.50. Ingmire.

ORIGINAL GRANTEE, PATENTEE. Part 1 Austin County, Texas Land Titles, Part 2 Bandera County Land Titles. Compiled by F. T. Ingmire and R.L. Thompson. St. Louis, 1979. 31p., index, 4to, pc. $6.95. Ingmire.

BAILEY

Created from Bexar County in 1876, one of fifty-four Panhandle counties created that year by the legislature. Organized in 1917, named for Peter J. Bailey, who died at the Alamo. County seat Muleshoe; other towns include Maple, Enochs, and Bula. Bounded by Cochran,Hockley,Lamb and Parmer Counties, and by New Mexico.

EARLY BAILEY COUNTY HISTORY. Paleo-Man to Plow-Man. By Muleshoe Jr. High Historical Society. Muleshoe,Tx., 1978. 150p., ill., biblio.,index, 4to. $15.00. Rudd.

BANDERA

Created from Bexar County and organized in 1856, named for Bandera " Flag " Mountains. County seat Bandera; other towns include Pipe Creek, Medina and Lake Hills. Bounded by Bexar, Kendall, Kerr, Real, Uvalde and Medina Counties.

ORIGINAL GRANTEE, PATENTEE. Part 1 Austin County,Texas Land Titles. Part 2 Bandera County, Texas Land Titles. Compiled by F. T. Ingmire. St. Louis, 1979. 31p., index, 4to.,pc. $6.95. Ingmire.

BASTROP

Created 1836, organized 1837, named for Felipe Enrique Neri, Baron de Bastrop. County seat Bastrop; other towns include Smithville and Elgin. Bounded by Travis,Williamson, Lee, Fayette,Gonzales and Caldwell Counties.

AUSTIN COLONY PIONEERS. Including history of Bastrop, Fayette, Grimes, Montgomery and Washington Counties. By Worth S. Ray. Austin, 1970. Reprint of 1949 ed. 378p., ill.,index. $17.50. Ranger.

BASTROP COUNTY CENSUS RECORDS 1850. $13.00. Heritage.

BASTROP COUNTY 1691-1900. By Bill Moore. Burnet, Tx., revised ed., 322p., ill.,index. $14.95. Ranger.

ELGIN. A History of Elgin, Texas 1872-1972. Compiled by Members of the Elgin Historical Committee. Elgin, Tx.,1972, 168p.,ill., paper $3.15, cloth $5.25. Elgin.

HISTORY OF ST. JOHN LUTHERAN CHURCH PAIGE, TEXAS. 1979. 24p., ill.,pc. $3.50. Laake.

ORIGINAL GRANTEE, PATENTEE. Armstrong County, Texas Land Titles. Bastrop County, Texas Land Titles. Compiled by F. T. Ingmire and R.L. Thompson. St. Louis, 1979. 30p.,index, 4to, pc. $6.95. Ingmire.

RECOLLECTIONS OF EARLY TEXAS. Memoirs of John Holland Jenkins. By John H. Jenkins III. Austin, 1958. Later printing. 333p., ill., biblio.,index. $15.00. Ranger.

TEXAS CENSUS 1850 Vol.8. Compiled by V.K. Carpenter. 1979. Reprint ed. pc. $10.00. Presley.

BAYLOR

Created from Fannin County 1858, organized 1879, named for Texas Ranger Henry W. Baylor. County seat Seymour; other towns include Red Springs and Westover. Bounded by Wilbarger, Wichita, Archer, Young, Throckmorton, Haskell, Knox and Foard Counties.

BAYLOR COUNTY, TEXAS LAND TITLES. Compiled by F.T. Ingmire and R.L. Thompson. St. Louis, 1979. 21p., index, 4to, pc. $6.95. Ingmire.

SALT PORK TO SIRLOIN. The History of Baylor County from 1879 to 1930. By Baylor County Historical Society. Quanah, 1972. 2d Ed. 174p., ill. 4to. $25.00. Ranger.

BEE

Created from Karnes, Live Oak, Goliad, Refugio and San Patricio Counties 1857, organized 1858, named for Republic of Texas statesman Barnard E. Bee. County seat Beeville; other towns include Skidmore and Pettus. Bounded by Karnes, Live Oak, Goliad, Refugio and San Patricio Counties.

THE HISTORICAL STORY OF BEE COUNTY, TEXAS. By Camp Ezell. Beeville,Tx., 1973, 258p.,ill. $10.00. Beeville.

ORIGINAL GRANTEE,PATENTEE. Bee County, Texas Land Titles, Borden County, Texas Land Titles. Compiled by F.T. Ingmire and R.L. Thompson. St. Louis, 1979, 30p., index, 4to, pc. $6.95. Ingmire.

BELL

Created from Milam County and organized 1850, named for Texas Governor Peter H. Bell. County seat Belton; other towns include Temple, Killeen, Harker Heights, Salado, Bartlett and Holland. Bounded by Burnet, Lampasas, Coryell, McLennan, Falls, Milam & Williamson Counties.

BELL COUNTY, TEXAS LAND TITLES. Compiled by F.T. Ingmire and R.L. Thompson. St. Louis, 1979. 39p., index, 4to. pc. $6.95. Ingmire.

EARLY DAYS IN CENTRAL TEXAS. By F.M. Cross. 1914. Reprint ed. $5.00. Bell.

HI NEIGHBOR! By Madie B. Smith. $3.95. Temple.

A HISTORY OF BELL COUNTY. By Bertha Atkinson. 1929. Reprint ed. 139p. pc. $5.00. Bell.

LITTLE FLOCK CEMETERY. BELL COUNTY, TEXAS. Compiled by W.B. Zatopek. 1982. 39p., index. $10.00. Zatopek.

BEXAR

Created 1836, organized 1837, named for son of Duke of Bexar. County seat San Antonio; other towns include Selma, Elmendorf, Converse, Kirby, Schertz, Alamo Heights and Universal City. Bounded by Comal, Kendall, Bandera, Medina, Atascosa, Wilson and Guadalupe Counties.

BEXAR COUNTY CENSUS RECORDS 1850. $35.00. Heritage.

COMPREHENSIVE SURNAME INDEX TO " WITH THE MAKERS OF SAN ANTONIO" BY FREDERICK C. CHABOT. $8.00. Schiess.

THE DOCTORS HERFF. A Three Generation Memoir. By F.P. Herff. San Antonio, 1973. Two volumes, 519p., ill., index. $18.00. Ranger.

THE FALL OF THE ALAMO. By Reuben M. Potter, introduction by Charles Grosvenor. $10.00. Grosvenor.

GENTILZ. Artist of the Old Southwest. By D.S. Kendall. Austin, 1974. 127p., ill., biblio., index. $20.00. Ranger.

HISTORY, BATTLES AND FALL OF THE ALAMO. With points of interest, etc., of San Antonio, Texas. (San Antonio, 1896) Reprint of 1980. 34p., ill., pc. $5.50. Ranger.

IN RE RICARDO RODRIGUEZ. An attempt at Chicano Disfranchisement in San Antonio 1896-1897. By Arnoldo De Leon. San Antonio, 1979. 16p., notes, pc. Write. Angelo.

JAMES P. NEWCOMB. Texas Journalist and Political Leader. By John Fowler. Austin, (1976) 130p., biblio., pc. $4.00. DJ

THE MISSIONS OF SAN ANTONIO. By Fritz A. Toepperwein. Boerne, 1976, 16p., ill., pc, $2.00. Highland.

ORIGIN AND FALL OF THE ALAMO. By John S. Ford. San Antonio, 1900. Reprint of 1980. 38p., ill., pc. $5.50. Ranger.

ORIGINAL PATENTEE, GRANTEE. Bexar County, Texas Land Titles. Compiled by F.T. Ingmire. pc. $8.95. Ingmire.

OUR FAMILY HERITAGE. By A.F. Deuvall & P.A. Rodriguez. San Antonio, 1975. 203p., ill., index, pc. $15.00. Deuvall.

SAN ANTONIO. A Historical Portrait. By John L. Davis. Austin, 1978. 183p., ill., biblio. $20.00. Ranger.

SAN ANTONIO. A Historical and Pictorial Guide. By Charles H. Ramsdell. Austin, 1976. Revised ed. 311p., pc. $5.95. Ranger.

SAN ANTONIO IN THE 18TH CENTURY. By San Antonio Bicentennial Heritage Committee. San Antonio. 154p., $7.95. Ranger.

SAN ANTONIO LEGACY. By Donald E. Everett. San Antonio, 1979. 121p., ill. $10.00. Ranger.

THE SAN ANTONIO RIVER. By Fritz A. Toepperwein. Boerne, Tx., 2d Ptg., 17p., ill., pc. $2.00. Highland.

SAN ANTONIO WAS. Seen Through a Magic Lantern. By Cecilia Steinfeldt. San Antonio, 1978. 204p.,ill., paper $14.95, Hardcover $21.95 San Antonio.

STONE BELLS, LIGHTED CANDLES. Memories of the Old Ursuline Academy at the Turn of the Century. By Emily Edwards. San Antonio, 1981. $6.27. Alamo.

TEXAS CENSUS 1850. Vol. 7. Compiled by V.K. Carpenter. 1979. Reprint ed. pc. $10.00. Presley.

TRINITY UNIVERSITY. A Record of One Hundred Years. By Donald E. Everett. San Antonio, 1968. 276p., $5.00. Ranger.

"THE WILD AND FREE DUKEDOM OF BEXAR". By Elton Cude. San Antonio, 1978. 377p.,ill.,biblio.,index. $20.00. Ranger.

YANAGUANA'S SUCCESSORS. The story of the Canary Islanders' immigration into Texas in the 18th Century. By Samuel M. Buck. San Antonio, 1980. 250th Ann. Comm. Ed. 302p., ill.,index. $15.00.Alcalde.

Periodical: A.L.A.M.O. Publication of the Alamo Lore and Myth Organization. $15.00/year with membership. Waters.

Periodical. OUR HERITAGE . Publication of the San Antonio Genealogical and Historical Society. $4 ea. San.

BLANCO

Created from Burnet, Comal, Gillespie and Hays Counties and organized 1858, named for Blanco ("white") River. County seat Johnson City; other towns include Blanco and Twin Sisters. Bounded by Gillespie, Llano, Burnet, Travis, Hays, Comal and Kendall Counties.

BLANCO COUNTY FAMILIES. For One Hundred Years. By John S. Moursand. edited and revised by Mabel Stribling. Burnet. 1981. Originially published in 1958. 492p., ill., $25.00. Ranger.

BLANCO COUNTY HISTORY. By John S. Moursand. Burnet,1979, 613p., bibliog. $25.00. Ranger.

MEMOIRS OF A TEXAS PIONEER GRANDMOTHER 1805-1915. By Ottilie F. Goeth. Burnet,Tx., 1982. 2d Ed. Revised. 260p., ill., biblio., index. $15.00. Ranger.

ORIGINAL GRANTEE, PATENTEE. Part I Calhoun County, Texas Land Titles. Part II Blanco County Texas Land Titles. Compiled by F.T. Ingmire. St. Louis, 4to. pc. $8.95. Ingmire.

SECOND FATHERLAND: The Life and Fortunes of a German Immigrant. By Max Krueger. ed. by M.M. Sibley. College Station,Tx 1976, 186p.,ill. $12.00. Ranger.

BORDEN

Created from Bexar County 1876, organized 1891, named for Gail Borden, Jr. County seat Gail and only town. Bounded by Lynn, Garza, Dawson, Scurry, Mitchell, Howard and Martin Counties.

ORIGINAL GRANTEE, PATENTEE. Bee County, Texas Land Titles, Borden County, Texas Land Titles. Compiled by F.T. Ingmire and R.L. Thompson. St. Louis, 1979. 30p., index, 4to, pc. $6.95. Ingmire.

BOSQUE

Created from Milam Land District and McLennan County and organized 1854, named for Bosque ("woods") River. County seat Meridian; other towns include Iredell, Clifton, Valley Mills and Cranfills Gap. Bounded by Somervell, Erath, Hamilton, Coryell, McLennan, Hill and Johnson Counties.

BOSQUE COUNTY, TEXAS MARRIAGE RECORDS 1860-1890. Compiled by F.T. Ingmire. St. Louis, 1981, 64p.,index, 4to. $11.95. Ingmire.

BOWIE

Created from Red River County and organized 1840, named for James Bowie. County seat Boston; other towns include Texarkana, New Boston, Redwater, Hooks and Nash. Bounded by Red River, Morris and Cass Counties, by Arkansas on the East and Oklahoma on the north.

BOWIE COUNTY, TEXAS BASIC BACKGROUND BOOK. Genealogical Reference Material. Texarkana, 1980, 110p., map, 4to, paper $35.00, Hardcover, $45.00. Scheffelin.

BOWIE COUNTY, TEXAS HISTORICAL HANDBOOK. Compiled by Mrs. N.W. Jennings and Mrs. E.E. Varner. Texarkana, 1976. 60p., ill. index, 4to, pc. $2.50. Texarkana.

BOWIE COUNTY CENSUS RECORDS 1850. Index. $8.00. Heritage.

BOWIE COUNTY, TEXAS FEDERAL CENSUS FOR 1850. Texarkana, Tx., 28p., 4to, pc. $8.00. TUGS.

BOWIE COUNTY, TEXAS FEDERAL CENSUS FOR 1860. Texarkana, Tx., 38p., index, pc. $10.00. TUGS.

BOWIE COUNTY, TEXAS FEDERAL CENSUS FOR 1870. Texarkana, Tx., 58p., index, 4to, pc. $12.00. TUGS.

TEXAS CENSUS 1850. Vol. 18. Compiled by V.K. Carpenter. 1979. Reprint ed. pc. $10.00. Presley.

Periodical: TEXARKANA, USA. Quarterly of the Texarkana USA Genealogical Society. Write. TUGS.

BRAZORIA

Created 1836, organized 1837, named for Brazos River. County seat Angleton; other towns include Freeport, Alvin, Lake Jackson, Clute, Pearland, Sweeney, West Columbia and Danbury. Bounded by Galveston, Harris, Fort Bend, Matagorda, and Wharton Counties and by the Gulf of Mexico.

BRAZORIA COUNTY CENSUS RECORDS 1850. Index. $9.00. Heritage.

BRAZORIA COUNTY, TEXAS CENSUS RECORDS 1860. Brazosport, 1978. 30p., 4to, pc. $4.00. Chaparral.

GHOSTS ALONG THE BRAZOS. By Mrs. Catherine Foster. $8.95 Brazoria.

HISTORICAL SCRAPBOOK OF WEST COLUMBIA, TEXAS. Angleton, map, pc. $5.00. Brazoria.

INVENTORY OF COUNTY RECORDS, BRAZORIA COUNTY COURTHOUSE, ANGLETON, TEXAS. Compiled by James E. Riney, et al. Denton, Tx., 1980. Two vols. 247 & 175pp. index, 4to, pc. $6.00. TSL

MARRIAGE RECORDS OF BRAZORIA COUNTY 1829-1870. $10.00 Brazosport.

A NARRATIVE HISTORY OF BRAZORIA COUNTY, TEXAS. By James A. Creighton. Angleton, 1975. 533p., ill. $17.50. Brazoria.

THE OLD PLANTATIONS AND THEIR OWNERS OF BRAZORIA COUNTY. By Abner J. Strobel. Austin, 1979. Reprint of 1926 ed. 46p., frontis., pc. $5.50. Ranger.

PEACH POINT PLANTATION. The first 150 years. By Marie Beth Jones. Angleton, Tx. $15.00. Peach.

TEXAS CENSUS 1850. Vol. 2. Compiled by V.K. Carpenter. 1979. Reprint. ed. pc. $10.00. Presley.

BRAZOS

Created from Robertson and Washington Counties 1841, organized 1843, named for Brazos River. County seat Bryan; other towns include College Station and Harvey. Bounded by Robertson, Burleson, Madison, Grimes and Leon Counties.

BRAZOS COUNTY, TEXAS CENSUS RECORDS 1850. $4.50. Heritage.

A CENTENNIAL HISTORY OF TEXAS A. & M. UNIVERSITY, 1876-1976. By Henry C. Dethloff. College Station, Tx. 1975. Two volumes. 744p., $25.00. Ranger.

A PICTORIAL HISTORY OF TEXAS A. & M. UNIVERSITY, 1876-1976. By Henry C. Dethloff. College Station, Tx. 1975. 232p., ill. 4to. $15.00. Ranger.

TEXAS CENSUS 1850. Vol. 9. Compiled by V.K. Carpenter. 1979. Reprint ed. pc. $10.00. Presley.

Periodical: THE BRAZOS VALLEY ADVERTISER. Publication of the Brazos Genealogical Association. $10/year. Brazos.

BREWSTER

Created from Presidio County and organized 1887, named for Texas soldier, jurist and statesman Henry P. Brewster. County seat Alpine; other towns include Marathon and Terlingua. Bounded by Presidio, Jeff Davis, Pecos and Terrell Counties, and by Mexico on the south.

ALPINE, TEXAS. Then and Now. By Dr. Clifford B. Casey. Seagraves, 1981. 437p., ill., 4to. $20.00. Ranger.

THE BIG BEND. A History of the Last Texas Frontier. By Ron Tyler. 288p., ill., pc. $5.75. Ranger.

BIG BEND. A Homesteader's Story. By J.O. Langford with Fred Gipson. Austin, 1952. Reissue, 1974. 191p., ill., index, pc. $7.95. Ranger.

BIG BEND NATIONAL PARK. The Formative Years. By John R. Jameson. El Paso, pc. $3.00. Ranger.

THE BIG BEND OF THE RIO GRANDE. A Guide to the Rocks, Landscape, Geologic History and Settlers of the Area of the Big Bend National Park. By R.A. Maxwell. Austin, 1968. Reprint ed. 138p., ill. pc. $3.00. BEG.

CHRONICLES OF THE BIG BEND. A Photographic Memoir of Life on the Border. By W.D. Smithers. Austin, 1976. 144p.,ill., index, tall 8vo. $14.00. Ranger.

EARLY TRAIL DRIVES IN THE BIG BEND. By W.D. Smithers. El Paso, 1979, 32p.,ill.,pc. $3.00. Ranger.

MIRAGES, MYSTERIES AND REALITY. Brewster County, Texas, The Big Bend of the Rio Grande. Seagraves,Tx., 1972. 2d Ptg., 485p. ill.,4to. $12.50. Ranger.

QUICKSILVER. Terlingua and the Chisos Mining Company. By Kenneth B. Ragsdale. College Station,Tx., 1976. 368p., ill.,$14.50. Ranger.

SUL ROSS STATE UNIVERSITY 1917-1975. By Clifford B. Casey. Seagraves,Tx. $13.50. Ranger.

TALES OF THE BIG BEND. By Elton Miles. College Station,Tx. 1976. 189p., ill.,biblio.,index. $10.00. Ranger.

THE WAY I HEARD IT. Tales of the Big Bend. By Walter Fulcher. Austin, 1973. 2d Ed. 87p.,ill. $7.50. Ranger.

BRISCOE

Created from Bexar County 1876, organized 1882, named for Republic of Texas soldier Andrew Briscoe. County seat Silverton, another town is Quitaque. Bounded by Armstrong, Donley, Hall, Motley, Floyd, and Swisher Counties.

FOOTPRINTS OF TIME 1876-1976. History of Briscoe County, Texas. Dallas, 1976. 605p., $42.40. Briscoe.

BROOKS

Created from Hidalgo, Starr and Zapata Counties and organized in 1911, named for Texas Ranger-politician James A. Brooks. County seat Falfurrias; other towns include Encino and Rachal. Bounded by Jim Wells, Kenedy, Duval, Jim Hogg, Starr and Hidalgo Counties.

No publications located.

BROWN

Created 1856 from Comanche and Travis Counties, organized 1857, named for early Texas settler Henry S. Brown. County seat Brownwood; other towns include Bangs, Zephyr, Early and Blanket. Bounded by Coleman, Callahan, Eastland, Comanche, Mills, McCulloch and San Saba Counties.

EARLY COMMUNITIES OF LAKE BROWNWOOD. By P.L.C. Weedon. 1980. Revised ed. 145p.,index, pc. $20.00. Byrd.

FRONTIER'S GENERATION. The History of Brown County, Texas. By Tevis Clyde Smith. 1931. Recent reprint ed. $7.50. Ericson.

HISTORY OF FIRST BAPTIST CHURCH. Brownwood,Tx. $10.00 Coursey.

THE PROMISED LAND. A History of Brown County, Texas. By James C. White. Brownwood,Tx. 1941. 1st Ptg. 123p.,index,pc. $25.00. Ranger.

RURAL CEMETERY INSCRIPTIONS, BROWN COUNTY TEXAS. Compiled by H.E. Wetzel. 1980, 301p.,map, 4to, pc. $16.50. Wetzel.

ZEPHYR, YESTERDAY AND TODAY. With 120 Genealogies of Zephyr's Pioneer Families. 1980. 264p.,pc. $10.00. Zephyr.

BURLESON

Created and organized 1846 from Milam and Washington Counties, named for Texas Revolutionary Edward Burleson. County seat Caldwell; other towns include Snook, Lyons and Somerville. Bounded by Milam, Brazos, Lee, Washington, Robertson Counties.

ASTRIDE THE OLD SAN ANTONIO ROAD. A History of Burleson County, Texas. Caldwell, 1980, 513p.,ill.,biblio.,index. $35.00.Burleson.

BURLESON COUNTY CENSUS RECORDS 1850. Index. $7.00.Heritage.

TEXAS CENSUS 1850. Vol. 9. Compiled by V.K. Carpenter. 1979. Reprint ed.,pc. $10.00. Presley.

BURNET

Created 1852 from Bell, Travis and Williamson Counties, organized 1854, named for Texas Provisional President David G. Burnet. County seat Burnet; other towns include Bertram, Granite Shoals, Marble Falls and Lake Victor. Bounded by Blanco, Llano, San Saba, Lampasas, Bell, Williamson and Travis Counties.

BURNET COUNTY HISTORY. By Darrell Debo. Burnet, 1979. Two Volumes. 390 & 354pp.,ill.,index, 4to. $50.00. Ranger.

THE LAKE VICTOR STORY. By Maurice C. Shelby. 1972. 2d Ptg. 208p.,ill. $17.50. Ranger.

CALDWELL

Created and organized from Gonzales and Bastrop Counties 1848, and supposedly named for Mathew "Old Paint" Caldwell. County seat Lockhart; other towns include Luling and Martindale. Bounded by Hays, Travis, Bastrop, Fayette, Gonzales and Guadalupe Counties.

CALDWELL COUNTY CENSUS RECORDS 1850. index.$6.50.Heritage.

HISTORICAL LOCKHART. Then and Now. By Zona A. Withers. Lockhart,Tx. 1981. Two volumes, pc. $3.00 each. Withers.

ORIGINAL GRANTEE, PATENTEE. Part I Callahan County Land Titles. Part II Caldwell County Land Titles. Part III Cameron County Land Titles. Compiled by F.T. Ingmire. St. Louis. $8.95. Ingmire.

TEXAS CENSUS 1850. Vol. 8. Compiled by V.K. Carpenter. 1979. Reprint Ed. pc. $10.00. Presley.

CALHOUN

Created from Victoria, Jackson and Matagorda Counties and organized 1846, named for South Carolina's John Caldwell Calhoun. County seat Port Lavaca; other towns include Point Comfort, Port O'Connor, Seadrift and Indianola. Bounded by Jackson, Victoria, Refugio, Aransas and Matagorda Counties and the Gulf of Mexico.

LOOKING BACK. A Scrapbook of Calhoun County. By Paul Freier. Port Lavaca, Tx, 1979, 290p.,ill., index, 4to, $17.50. Freier.

ORIGINAL GRANTEE, PATENTEE. Part I Calhoun County, Texas Land Titles Part II Blanco County, Texas Land Titles. Compiled by F.T. Ingmire. St. Louis, $8.95. Ingmire.

CALHOUN COUNTY CENSUS RECORDS 1850. $6.00. Heritage.

CALHOUN COUNTY, TEXAS 1850 CENSUS. 64p., index, pc. $10.00. McCown.

TEXAS CENSUS 1850. Vol. 2. Compiled by V.K. Carpenter. 1979 Reprint ed., pc. $10.00. Presley.

CALHOUN COUNTY, TEXAS 1860 CENSUS. 118p.,index,pc.$10.00 McCown.

CALHOUN COUNTY, TEXAS 1870 CENSUS. 184p.,index,pc.$15.00 McCown.

CALHOUN COUNTY, TEXAS 1880 CENSUS. 138p.,index,pc.$10.00 McCown.

CALHOUN COUNTY, TEXAS 1900 CENSUS.In preparation.McCown.

Periodical: KARANKAWA KOUNTRY. Quarterly of the Calhoun County Genealogical Society. $10/Year. Calhoun.

CALLAHAN

Created from Bexar, Bosque and Travis Counties 1858, organized 1877, named for Texas Ranger James H. Callahan. County seat Baird; other towns include Putnam, Clyde and Cross Plains. Bounded by Shackelford, Eastland, Brown, Coleman, Taylor and Jones Counties.

EARLY DAYS IN CALLAHAN COUNTY. By B.C. Chrisman.$9.95. APS.

INVENTORY OF COUNTY RECORDS, CALLAHAN COUNTY COURTHOUSE BAIRD, TEXAS. Compiled by Fane Downs,et al. Denton, 1977. 151p., map, index. 4to.pc. $1.00. TSL.

ORIGINAL GRANTEE, PATENTEE. Part I. Callahan County,Texas Land Titles. Part II. Caldwell County, Texas Land Titles. Part III. Cameron County, Texas Land Titles. Compiled by F.T. Ingmire. St. Louis. $8.95. Ingmire.

CAMERON

Created and organized from Nueces County 1848, named for Mier Expedition leader Captain Ewen Cameron. County seal Brownsville; other towns include Harlingen, San Benito, Port Isabel, Rio Hondo, La Feria, Bounded by Hidalgo and Willacy Counties, by Mexico on the South and the Gulf of Mexico on the east.

A CENTURY OF SERVICE. History of the Diocese of Brownsville. By Gilbert R. & M.O. Cruz. 1979. $2.00. Diocese.

HISTORICAL BROWNSVILLE. Original Townsite Guide. By Betty Bay. Brownsville, 1980. 202p.,ill.,pc. $10.00. Brownsville.

ORIGINAL GRANTEE, PATENTEE. Part I. Callahan County, Texas Land Titles. Part II. Caldwell County, Texas Land Titles. Part III. Cameron County, Texas Land Titles. Compiled by F.T. Ingmire. St. Louis. $8.95. Ingmire.

TEXAS CENSUS 1850. Vol. I. Compiled by V.K. Carpenter. 1979 Reprint ed. pc. $10.00. Presley.

THE TWIN CITIES OF THE BORDER AND THE COUNTRY OF THE LOWER RIO GRANDE. By Lieutenant W.H. Chatfield. New Orleans, 1893. Reprint of Brownsville Historical Association, 1959. 48p, ill.,map, folio, pc. $5.00. Brownsville.

Periodical: GENEALOGICAL TIPS. Publication of the Tip-O'-Texas Genealogical Society. Write. Tip.

CAMP

Created from Upshur County and organized 1874, named for soldier-jurist John L. Camp. County seat Pittsburg; other towns include Leesburg and Newsome. Bounded by Titus, Morris, Upshur, Wood and Franklin Counties.

INVENTORY OF COUNTY RECORDS, CAMP COUNTY COURTHOUSE PITTSBURG, TEXAS. Compiled by Douglas Ferrier, et al. Denton, Tx 1977. 135p.,map,4to.,pc. $1.00. TSL.

CARSON

Created from Bexar County 1876, organized 1888, named for Republic of Texas politician-businessman Samuel Price Carson. County seat Panhandle; other towns include White Deer, Groom, Skellytown and Pantex. Bounded by Hutchinson, Roberts, Gray, Donley, Armstrong, Randall, Potter and Moore Counties.

A TIME TO PURPOSE. A Chronicle of Carson County. Edited by Mrs. R.E. Randel. 1966-1972. Four volumes, ill., 4to. $200.00. Carson.

CASS

Created from Bowie County and organized 1846, named for Michigan Senator Lewis Cass. County seat Linden; other towns include Atlanta, Avinger, Bloomberg, Queen City and Hughes Springs. Bounded by Bowie, Morris and Marion Counties, and by Arkansas and Louisiana on the east.

THE BEST DAMN TEACHER. By L.L. Lloyd. Cisco, Tx, 1978. Includes teaching in Queen City. $9.95. Lloyd.

CASS COUNTY CEMETERIES. 275p.,paper $15.50, hardcover $19.50. Cass.

CASS COUNTY CENSUS RECORDS 1850. Index. $18.00. Heritage.

CASS COUNTY PEDIGREE BOOK. Index. $6.00. Cass.

CASS COUNTY, TEXAS MARRIAGE RECORDS 1847-1880. Books I through 4. Compiled by F.T. Ingmire. St. Louis, 1981. 62p., index. pc. $11.95. Ingmire.

HISTORY OF CASS COUNTY PEOPLE. In Preparation. Cass.

LAWS CHAPEL. A History and Records. 1853-1876. $4.00. Cass.

PEOPLE OF CASS COUNTY AND QUEEN CITY. Vol. I $10.00, Vol. II $8.00. Bowman.

QUEEN CITY, TEXAS 1876-1976. $10.00. Bowman.

TEXAS CENSUS 1850. Vol. 18. 1979 reprint ed. pc. $10.00. Presley.

Periodical: CASS COUNTY GENEALOGICAL SOCIETY QUARTERLY. $7/Year with membership. Cass.

CASTRO

Created from Bexar County 1876, organized 1891, named for Portuguese colonizer Henri Castro. County seat Dimmitt; other towns include Hart, Easter and Nazareth. Bounded by Deaf Smith, Randall, Swisher, Hale, Lamb and Parmer Counties.

CASTRO COUNTY TEXAS 1891-1891. Dimmitt,Tx.,1981. 560p., ill.,index. $45.00. Castro.

HISTORY OF THE FIRST SEVENTY-FIVE YEARS OF CASTRO COUNTY, TEXAS 1891-1966. Dimmitt,Tx., 1966. 64p.,ill.,4to.,pc. $15.00. Ranger.

THIS LAND WE HOLD. By Mrs. L.B. Bowden.History of Sunnyside. 1971. 400p.. $12.95. Bowden.

CHAMBERS

Created and organized 1858 from Liberty and Jefferson Counties, named for Texas Revolution activist Thomas Jefferson Chambers. County seat Anahuac; other towns include Winnie, Stowell, Beach City and Mont Belvieu. Bounded by Jefferson, Harris and Galveston Counties and by the Gulf of Mexico.

ANAHUAC IN 1832. The Cradle of the Texas Revolution. By Margaret Henson. Anahuac, Tx., 1982, 44p.,pc. $3.50. Battle.

BOARD OF LAND COMMISSIONERS, HARRISBURG DISTRICT, 1838. 158p., 4to,pc. $20.00. Chambers.

CHAMBERS COUNTY, TEXAS CEMETERIES. Compiled by Mrs. M.S. Wright & Zelma H. Wright,Jr. Decorah,Iowa. 1975, 89p.,ill.,index, 4to. $10.50. Southeast.

CHAMBERS COUNTY, TEXAS CENSUS 1870. Compiled by F.D. Bueckner. 35p., index, pc. $4.00. Chaparral.

DIAMOND IN THE ROUGH. A History of Cove, Texas. Volume I 1824-1900. Baytown,Tx. 1981. 118p., biblio.,index, 4to.pc. $12.50. Clark.

1859 TAX ROLL FOR CHAMBERS COUNTY, TEXAS. 21p.,4to. pc. $5.00. Chambers.

A HISTORY OF CHAMBERS COUNTY,TEXAS. Vol I. By J.H. Harry. Dallas, 1981. Originally pub. 1940. 230p., biblio.,index, $20.00. Chambers.

INDEX TO 1900 CHAMBERS COUNTY CENSUS. 28p., 4to. pc., $5.00. Chambers.

1870 FEDERAL CENSUS FOR CHAMBERS COUNTY, TEXAS. 89p. 4to. $12.50. Chambers.

1900 CENSUS FOR CHAMBERS COUNTY, TEXAS, 204p., 4to., pc. $30.00. Chambers.

CHEROKEE

Created and organized from Nacogdoches County 1846, named for the Cherokee Indians. County seat Rusk; other towns include Jacksonville,

Bullard, Troup, Alto and Wells. Bounded by Smith, Henderson, Rusk, Anderson, Houston, Angelina and Nacogdoches Counties.

BULLARD. Its History and People. By Bullard Community Library Association. $20.00. Bullard.

CEMETERY RECORDS OF CHEROKEE COUNTY, TEXAS. By Helen W. Crawford. Jacksonville, Tx, 1971-74. 4to, pc. Five volumes covering various parts of the county. Prices from $10-$15 per volume. Crawford.

CHEROKEE COUNTY CENSUS RECORDS 1850. Index. $31.00 Heritage.

TEXAS CENSUS 1850. Vol II. Compiled by V.K. Carpenter. 1979 Reprint ed. pc. $10.00. Presley.

1860 CENSUS, CHEROKEE COUNTY, TEXAS. Compiled by Ogreta Huttash & Mildred Smith. $16.00. Huttash.

1870 FEDERAL CENSUS, CHEROKEE COUNTY, TEXAS. Compiled by Helen Crawford. $17.50. Huttash.

CHEROKEE COUNTY, TEXAS CENSUS 1880. $25.00. Cherokee.

SURNAME INDEX 1880 CHEROKEE COUNTY, TEXAS CENSUS. $3.50. Chaparral.

CIVIL WAR RECORDS OF CHEROKEE COUNTY, TEXAS. Vol.I. Compiled by Ogreta W. Huttash. 93p., 4to. pc. $12.50. Ericson.

HISTORICAL MARKERS OF CHEROKEE COUNTY, TEXAS. Compiled by Ogreta W. Huttash. 32p., 4to, pc. $7.50. Ericson.

MARRIAGE RECORDS OF CHEROKEE COUNTY, TEXAS. Compiled by Ogreta W. Huttash. Vol. I 1846-1880, Vol. 2 1881-1905. Jacksonville, Tx 1973. 4to. $12.95 each volume. Huttash.

CHILDRESS

Created from Bexar County 1876, organized 1887, named for George Campbell Childress, author of the Texas Declaration of Independence. County seat Childress, which has more than 95% of county's population. Bounded by Hall, Cottle, Hardeman and Collingsworth Counties, and by Oklahoma on part of east border.

THE CHILDRESS COUNTY HERITAGE. Projected for publication in 1983. Price unknown. Childress.

CLAY

Created and organized from Cooke County 1857, reorganized 1873, named for Henry Clay. County seat Henrietta; other towns include Bluegrove, Bellevue, Byers and Petrolia. Bounded by Montague, Jack, Archer and Wichita Counties, and by Oklahoma on the north.

CLAY COUNTY, TEXAS CEMETERIES. Compiled by Walter F. Speakman. 300p. Unbound $15.00, Hardcover $27.50. TSGS.

A HISTORY OF CLAY COUNTY. By W.C. Taylor. Austin, 1972 168p., ill.,biblio.,index. $12.50. Ranger.

COCHRAN

Created 1876 from Bexar County, organized 1924, named for Alamo defender Robert Cochran. County seat Morton; other towns include

Whiteface and Bledsoe. Bounded by Bailey, Lamb, Hockley and Yoakum Counties, and by New Mexico on the west.

COCHRAN COUNTY "TEXAS LAST FRONTIER" Morton,Tx.,n.d. 5p typewritten. 4to. Free. Cochran.

COKE

Created and organized from Tom Green County 1859, named for Governor and U.S. Senator Richard Coke. County seat Robert Lee; other towns include Blackwell and Bronte. Bounded by Mitchell, Nolan, Tom Green, Runnels, and Sterling Counties.

INVENTORY OF COUNTY RECORDS, COKE COUNTY COURTHOUSE ROBERT LEE, TEXAS. Compiled by Mary Grace Sharp. Austin, 1975, 77p, index, 4to, pc. $1.00. TSL.

COLEMAN

Created from Brown and Travis Counties 1858, organized 1864, named for Sam Houston's aide-de-camp Colonel Robert E. Coleman. County seat Coleman; other towns include Santa Anna. Bounded by McCulloch, Taylor, Callahan, Brown, Concho and Runnels Counties.

COLEMAN COUNTY, TEXAS MARRIAGE RECORDS 1873-1890. Compiled by Reeves-Ingmire. $8.95. Ingmire.

DISCORD, TEXAS ON CAMP CREEK, and other stories. By G.N. Hunter. $10.00. Hunter.

FOUR YEARS IN THE COLEMAN JAIL, Daughter of Two Sheriffs. By Leona Bruce. 1982. 143p.,ill.,index. $12.00. Bruce.

SANTA ANNA'S PEAK. By Leona Bruce. Quanah,Tx, 1976. 175p. ill, biblio.,index. 4to. $20.00. Bruce.

COLLIN

Created and organized from Fannin County 1864, named for pioneer settler Collin McKinney, whose surname was chosen for the county seat. Other towns include Allen, Farmersville, Frisco, Plano, Richardson, Royse City and Wylie. Bounded by Grayson, Fannin, Hunt, Rockwall, Dallas and Denton Counties.

THE ANNALS OF ELDER HORN. Early Life in the Southwest. McKinney. 2d Ed. lst pub. in 1930. $8.50. Collin.

COLLIN COUNTY CENSUS RECORDS 1850. Index. $11.00. Heritage.

COLLIN COUNTY, TEXAS 1850 CENSUS. Richardson,Texas 47p., 4to, pc. $6.00. Bland.

TEXAS CENSUS 1850. Vol. 15. Compiled by V.K. Carpenter. 1979. Reprint ed. pc. $10.00. Presley.

COLLIN COUNTY, TEXAS 1860 CENSUS. Richardson,Tx. 131p., 4to, pc. $12.00. Bland.

COLLIN COUNTY, TEXAS CEMETERY INSCRIPTIONS. Compiled by Alice E. Pitts, et al. McKinney,Tx. Vol. I, 1975. $27.50. Vol. 2 1978. $19.25. Pitts.

COLLIN COUNTY, TEXAS LAND TITLES. Compiled by F.T. Ingmire and R.L. Thompson. St. Louis, 1979. 34p., index, 4to, pc., $6.95. Ingmire.

COLLIN COUNTY, TEXAS MARRIAGE RECORDS 1846-1876. McKinney, Tx. 1978. 65p., index. $12.95. Pitts.

RECORDS OF RECONSTRUCTION DAYS IN COLLIN COUNTY, TEXAS. 4to, pc. $10.00. Bland.

Periodical: COLLIN CHRONICLES. Quarterly publication of the Collin County Genealogical Society. $7.50/Year. CCGS.

COLLINGSWORTH

Created 1876 from Baylor and Young Counties, organized 1890, named for James Collinsworth, first Chief Justice of the Republic of Texas. County seat Wellington; other towns include Samnorwood. Bounded by Wheeler, Gray, Donley, Hall and Childress Counties and by Oklahoma on the east.

ARCHIBALD JOHN WRITES. The Rocking Chair Ranche Letters. By Estelle Tinker. Burnet, Tx 1979. 200p.,ill.,$9.95. Ranger.

COLORADO

Created 1836, organized 1837, named for Colorado River. County seat Columbus; other towns include Eagle Lake, Garwood and Weimer. Bounded by Fayette, Austin, Wharton, Jackson and Lavaca Counties.

COLORADO COUNTY CENSUS RECORDS 1850. Index. $9.50. Heritage.

COLUMBUS TEXAS SESQUICENTENNIAL 1823-1873. Compiled by Sesquicentennial Committee. Columbus, 1973. 52p.,ill., 4to.,pc. Price unknown, write. Columbus.

FLAMING FEUDS OF COLORADO COUNTY. By John W. Reese. Salado, 1962. 171p.,ill.,$15.00. Ranger.

TEXAS CENSUS 1850. Vol. 5. Compiled by V.K. Carpenter. 1979. Reprint ed. pc. $10.00. Presley.

COMAL

Created and organized from Bexar, Gonzales and Travis Counties 1846, named for Comal River. County seat New Braunfels; other towns include Canyon City. Bounded by Kendall, Blanco, Hays, Guadalupe & Bexar Counties.

COMAL COUNTY CENSUS RECORDS 1850. Index. $10.50. Heritage.

THE CYPRESS AND OTHER WRITINGS OF A GERMAN PIONEER IN TEXAS. By Herman Seele. Austin, 1979. 23lp.,ill. $12.95. Ranger.

THE HISTORY OF NEW BRAUNFELS AND COMAL COUNTY, TEXAS. By Oscar Haas. 1968. $11.00. Sophienburg.

LONE STAR AND DOUBLE EAGLE. Civil War Letters of a German-Texas Family. Edited by M.A. Goyne. Ft.Worth, 1982. 276p.,ill.,index, $15.00. Ranger.

TEXAS CENSUS 1850. Vol. 8. Compiled by V.K. Carpenter. 1979 Reprint ed. pc. $10.00. Presley.

COMANCHE

Created and organized from Bosque and Coryell Counties 1856, named for Comanche Indians. County seat Comanche; other towns include Proctor and DeLeon. Bounded by Eastland, Erath, Hamilton, Brown and Mills Counties.

COMANCHE COUNTY COURTHOUSES. An introduction to the Central Texas county of Comanche. By Frances B. Lockwood. Comanche, Tx., 1969. 22 unn. p., pc. $2.00. Comanche.

COMANCHE COUNTY, TEXAS CENSUS RECORDS. Compiled by W.I. Hudson & S.B. Cawyer. 91p., index, 4to. $10.00. Cawyer.

COMANCHE COUNTY, TEXAS GRAVESTONE INSCRIPTIONS. Compiled by Margaret Waring. Vol. I Rural Sites, 222p., index, 4to, pc. $20.00. Vol. 2 DeLeon and Area, 257p., index, 4to, pc. $18.00. Vol. 3. City of Comanche. 312p., index, 4to, pc. $20.00. Vol. 4, Remaining Rural Sites. In preparation. Waring.

PATCHWORK OF MEMORIES. Historical Sketches of Comanche County, Texas. By Heritage Division Committee. Comanche, 1976. 321p. ill. pc. $10.00. Ranger.

A PICTORIAL HISTORY OF DE LEON, TEXAS 1881-1981. Compiled by DeLeon Centennial Historical Committee. DeLeon, Tx. 1981. 178p., ill. 4to. $16.00. Weaver.

CONCHO

Created from Bexar County 1858, organized 1879, named for Concho ("shell") River. County seat Paint Rock; other towns include Eden and Eola. Bounded by Runnels, Coleman, McCulloch, Menard, Tom Green and Schleicher Counties.

No publications located.

COOKE

Created and organized from Fannin County 1846, named for Republic of Texas activist William G. Cooke. County seat Gainesville; other towns include Muenster, Valley View and Era. Bounded by Grayson, Denton, Wise and Montague Counties, and by Oklahoma on the north.

CEMETERY RECORDS OF COOKE COUNTY, TEXAS. Compiled by Cross Timbers Genealogical Society. 1980. 529p., $25.00. Morton.

COOKE COUNTY CENSUS RECORDS 1850. Index. $4.50. Heritage.

COOKE COUNTY, TEXAS. Where the South and the West Meet. By Michael Collins. 1981. 72p., ill., biblio., 4to., pc. $3.00. Morton.

COOKE COUNTY, TEXAS MARRIAGE RECORDS 1849-1879. Compiled by F.T. Ingmire. $6.95. Ingmire.

EARLY DAYS IN COOKE COUNTY. By C.N. Jones. 1977. Reprint of 1936 ed. 102p., pc. $3.00. Morton.

THE FIRST 100 YEARS IN COOKE COUNTY. By A. Morton Smith. 1955. Ed. of 1976. 290p., $12.95. Morton.

GEORGE WASHINGTON DIAMOND'S ACCOUNT OF THE GREAT HANGING AT GAINESVILLE, 1862. Ed. by Sam Acheson. Austin, 1963. 103p., frontis., index. pc. $3.50. Ranger.

THE GREAT HANGING AT GAINESVILLE,COOKE COUNTY,TEXAS OCTOBER, 1862, A.D.. By Thomas Barrett. Austin, 1961. Reprint of 1885 ed. 34p.,ill. paper $5, cloth $7.50. Ranger.

TEXAS CENSUS 1850. Vol. 16. Compiled by V.K. Carpenter. 1979. Reprint ed. pc. $10.00. Presley.

TEXAS: COOKE COUNTY. Its People, Productions, and Resources. By Cooke County Immigration Society. 1976. Reprint of 1889 ed. 32p., pc. $1.00. Morton.

CORYELL

Created and organized from Bell County 1854, named for Texas Ranger James Coryell. County seat Gatesville; other towns include Copperas Cove, Pearl, Purmela, Pancake, Turnersville, Evant and Fort Gates. Bounded by Hamilton, Bosque, McLennan, Bell and Lampasas Counties.

COPPERAS COVE. City of Five Hills. By Jerry K. Smith and P.D. McLaughlin. Burnet, 1980. 175p., ill.,biblio.,index, $12.00. Ranger.

FACTS & ANECDOTES OF TURNERSVILLE, TEXAS. By Laura A. Tharp. 224p., $7.35. Tharp.

HISTORY OF CORYELL COUNTY, TEXAS. By Zelma Scott. Austin, 1965. 278p., ill.,index. $12.50. Ranger.

HISTORY OF PEARL, TEXAS. By C.E. Freeman. 76p.,ill.,$10.00 Washburn.

HISTORY OF PURMELA, TEXAS. By Viola B. Cathey. ca. 1970. 80p., ill. $5.95. Cathey.

PANCAKE MEMORIES. By Viola Cathey. Copperas Cove,Tx. 1977. 100p.,ill.,pc. $5.95. Cathey.

VIGNETTES OF CORYELL COUNTY. By Clyde & Mabel Bailey. $7.95. Coryell.

Publication: CORYELL COUNTY GENEALOGICAL SOCIETY QUARTERLY. Write. Gatesville.

COTTLE

Created from Fannin County 1876, organized 1892, named for Alamo defender George Washington Cottle. County seat Paducah. Bounded by Hall, Childress, Hardeman, Foard, King, Dickens and Motley Counties.

COTTLE COUNTY MY DEAR. By Carmen Bennett., ill. $12.00 Paducah.

OUR ROOTS GROW DEEP. By Carmen Bennett.,ill. $12.00 Paducah.

CRANE

Created from Tom Green County 1887, organized 1927, named for Baylor University President William Carey Crane. County seat Crane; no other towns. Bounded by Ector,Upton,Crockett, Pecos and Ward Counties.

No publications located.

CROCKETT

Created from Bexar County 1875, organized 1891, named for David Crockett. County seat Ozona; no other towns. Bounded by Crane, Upton, Reagan, Irion, Sutton, Schleicher, Val Verde, Terrell, and Pecos Counties.

HISTORY OF CROCKETT COUNTY. By Crockett County Historical Society. San Angelo,Tx., 1976, 592p.,ill.,index.4to. $30.00. Crockett.

INVENTORY OF COUNTY RECORDS CROCKETT COUNTY COURTHOUSE OZONA, TEXAS. Compiled by Billy Jo Hayes,et al. Denton, Tx., 1977, 133p.,map, 4to, pc. $1.00. TSL.

YESTERYEARS IN OZONA AND CROCKETT COUNTY. By V.J. Pierce. Ozona,Tx. 1980. 137p., ill. $5.20. Crockett.

CROSBY

Created from Bexar County 1876, organized 1886, named for state official Stephen Crosby. County seat Crosbyton, other towns include Cone, Lorenzo and Ralls. Bounded by Hale, Floyd, Motley, Dickens, Kent, Garza, Lynn and Lubbock Counties.

CROSBY COUNTY HISTORY 1876-1879. $75.00. Crosby.

THE ESPUELA LAND AND CATTLE COMPANY. By W.C. Holden. Austin, 1970. 268p.,ill.,biblio.,index. $9.00. Ranger.

SUN RISING ON THE WEST. The Saga of Henry Clay and Elizabeth Smith. By W.H. Curry. Crosbyton,Tx. 1979. 306p.,ill.,bibl., index. 4to. $21.00. Crosby.

CULBERSON

Created from Bexar County 1876, organized 1912, named for Congressman David B. Culberson. County seat Van Horn; other towns include Lobo and Kent. Bounded by Reeves, Jeff Davis and Culberson Counties, and by New Mexico on the north.

HISTORY OF VAN HORN AND CULBERSON COUNTY. By Rosa Lee Wylie. Hereford, 1973. 183p.,ill. 4to. $8.50. Ranger.

DALLAM

Created from Bexar County 1876, organized 1891, named for editor-attorney James Wilmer Dallam. County seat Dalhart; other towns include Texline. Bounded by Sherman, Moore and Hartley Counties, by New Mexico on the west and Oklahoma on the north.

THE BOOK OF YEARS. A History of Dallam and Hartley Counties. By Lillie Mae Hunter. Hereford, 1969. 206p.,ill.,index. $12.50.Ranger.

DALLAS

Created and organized from Nacogdoches and Robertson Counties 1846, named for one of seven prominent people of that name. County seat

Dallas; other towns include Carrollton, Duncanville, Farmers Branch, Garland, Grand Prairie, Irving, Mesquite, Richardson, Duncanville, and De Soto. Bounded by Denton, Collin, Rockwall, Kaufman, Ellis, and Tarrant Counties.

ANCESTORS OF DALLAS GENEALOGICAL SOCIETY MEMBERS. Vol. I. Compiled by Dallas Genealogical Society. Dallas, 1978. 61p., index, 4to.,pc. $7.00. Dallas.

CEMETERY INSCRIPTIONS OF DALLAS COUNTY, TEXAS. Compiled by Dallas Genealogical Society. Announced for publication soon. Dallas.

DALLAS. The Deciding Years, A Historical Portrait. By A.C.Greene. Austin, 1973. 186p.,ill. $22.50 Ranger.

DALLAS COUNTY CENSUS RECORDS 1850. Index. $15.00. Heritage.

DALLAS, TEXAS. A Bibliographic Guide to the Sources of Its Social History. Austin, 1979. 64p., $6.95. Ranger.

DALLAS YESTERDAY. By Sam Acheson. Dallas, 1977. 425p.,port. index. $15.00. Ranger.

DIAPER DAYS OF DALLAS. By Ted Dealey. Dallas, 1966. Reprint ed. of 1975. 192p.,ill. $6.95. Ranger.

ELM FORK SETTLEMENTS. Farmers Branch and Carrollton. By G.M. Ogle. Quanah, 1977, 647p.,ill.,biblio.,index. $17.95. Ranger.

THE HISTORY OF CEDAR MOUNTAINS. By Mrs. L. Vinyard. 93p. $7.50. Duncanville.

HISTORY OF DALLAS COUNTY,TEXAS From 1837 to 1887. By J.H. Brown, and DALLAS COUNTY. A Record of its Pioneers and Progress. By John H. Cochran. Dallas, 1966, 115 & 296p. reprint of the 1887 and 1928 editions. $20.00. Ranger.

HISTORY OF DUNCANVILLE, TEXAS. 387p.,ill,index. $25.00 Duncanville.

INDEX TO PROBATE CASES-DALLAS COUNTY TEXAS (1846-1900). Compiled by Dallas Genealogical Society. Dallas, 1978, index. pc. $10.00. Dallas.

LISBON. West of the Trinity. By Helen B. Anthony. $6.95. Anthony.

MARRIAGES - DALLAS COUNTY TEXAS. Vol.1 Book A-E (1846-1877). Compiled by Dallas Genealogical Society. Dallas, 1978, index, 4to,pc.$10.00. Dallas.

MARRIAGE RECORDS OF DALLAS COUNTY TEXAS. Vol.2. Announced for publication soon. Dallas.

SANGERS'. Pioneer Texas Merchants. By Leon J. Rosenberg. Austin, 1978. 135p.,ill.,biblio.,index, $12.95. Ranger.

SOUTHERN METHODIST UNIVERSITY. Founding and Early Years. By Mary M.Thomas. Dallas, 1974. 236p.,ill.,biblio.,index,$12.50.Ranger.

TEXAS CENSUS 1850. Vol. 15. Compiled by V.K. Carpenter. 1979. Reprint ed. pc. $10.00. Presley.

THE UNIVERSITY OF TEXAS SOUTHWESTERN MEDICAL SCHOOL. Medical Education in Dallas 1900-1975. Dallas, 1976, 140p.,ill.,index, $10.00. Ranger.

Periodical: THE MESQUITE TREE. Quarterly of the Mesquite Historical and Genealogical Society. $8/Year. Mesquite.

Periodical: THE QUARTERLY.Publication of the Dallas Genealogical Society. $10/Year. Dallas.

Periodical: TEXAS KIN. Publication of the Dallas County East Genealogical Society. $6.00/Year. Dallas East.

DAWSON

Created from Bexar County 1876, organized 1905, named for Nicholas Mosby Dawson. County seat Lamesa; other towns include O'Donnell and Welch. Bounded by Terry, Lynn, Borden, Howard, Martin, Andrews and Gaines Counties.

DAWSON COUNTY HISTORY. The Tableland. By W. Smith and Ella Ward. Dallas, 1981, 624p., $42.00. Dawson.

Periodical: THREADS OF LIFE. Semi-annual publication of the Lamesa Area Genealogical Society. $3/Year. Lamesa.

DEAF SMITH

Created from Bexar County 1876, organized 1890, named for Erastus "Deaf" Smith, scout for Sam Houston. County seat Hereford; other towns include Dawn and Glen Rio. Bounded by Olham, Potter, Castro, Randall, and Parmer Counties, and by New Mexico on the west.

THE LAND AND ITS PEOPLE. By Deaf Smith County Historical Association. Lubbock, 1982. 664p.,$35.00. Hereford.

THE HEREFORD BRAND. The Belle of the Prairie Press. By Dudley Lynch. Austin, 1968. 68p.,biblio. pc. $4.00. DJ.

DELTA

Created and organized from Lamar and Hopkins Counties 1870, named for the Greek letter because of its triangular shape. County seat Cooper; other towns include Klondike. Bounded by Fannin, Lamar, Hopkins and Hunt Counties.

No publications located.

DENTON

Created and organized from Fannin County 1846, named for early minister-lawyer John B. Denton. County seat Denton; other towns include Coppell, Highland Village, Flower Mound, Lake Dallas and Lewisville. Bounded by Cooke, Grayson, Collin, Dallas, Tarrant, and Wise Counties.

DENTON COUNTY CENSUS RECORDS 1850. Index. $4.50. Heritage.

DENTON COUNTY, TEXAS MARRIAGE RECORDS 1875-1891. Compiled by F.T. Ingmire. $8.95. Ingmire.

HISTORY AND REMINISCENCES OF DENTON COUNTY. By E.F. Bates. Denton, 1918. Reprint ed. $15.00. Denton.

HISTORY OF DENTON, TEXAS. $15.75. Bridges.

INVENTORY OF COUNTY RECORDS, DENTON COUNTY COURTHOUSE DENTON,TEXAS. Compiled by Mary Pearson. Austin,Tx 1975. 111p.,index,4to,pc.$1.00. TSL.

THE JUSTIN STORY. By Grace Lee Parr. Quanah,Tx. 1976. 222p. ill.,$10.95. Ranger.

RECOLLECTIONS OF A TEXAS EDUCATOR. By L.H.Hubbard. Salado,1964.288p.,ill.$10.00. Fletcher.

TEXAS CENSUS 1850. Vol. 15. Compiled by V.K. Carpenter. 1979 Reprint ed. pc. $10.00. Presley.

DE WITT

Created and organized 1846 from Goliad, Gonzales and Victoria Counties, named for empresario Green C. DeWitt. County seat Cuero; other towns include Yoakum, Westhoff, Meyersville and Yorktown. Bounded by Karnes, Gonzales, Lavaca, Victoria and Goliad Counties.

DEWITT COLONY OF TEXAS. By Edward A. Lukes. Austin, 1976. 269p.,ill.,biblio.,index. $12.50. Ranger.

DEWITT COUNTY CENSUS RECORDS 1850. Index. $7.00. Heritage.

TEXAS CENSUS 1850. Vol. 2. Compiled by V.K. Carpenter. 1979. Reprint ed. pc. $10.00. Presley.

DICKENS

Created 1876 from Bexar County, organized 1891, named for Alamo soldier J. Dickens. County seat Dickens; other towns include Afton, McAdoo and Spur. Bounded by Crosby, Floyd, Motley, Cottle, King, Stonewall, Kent and Garza Counties.

THE ESPUELA LAND AND CATTLE COMPANY. By W.C. Holden. Austin,Tx. 1970, 268p.,ill.,biblio.,index. $9.00. Ranger.

DIMMIT

Created 1858 from Bexar, Uvalde, Maverick and Webb Counties, organized 1880, named for Philip Dimitt, co-author of the Goliad Declaration of Independence. County seat Carrizo Springs; other towns include Asherton, Big Wells and Catarina. Bounded by Maverick, Zavala, Frio, LaSalle and Webb Counties.

DIMMIT COUNTY-MESQUITE ROOTS. Vol. I. By Laura Tidwell, editor. 300p,ill.,biblio., announced for publication in 1983. Tidwell.

DONLEY

Created from Bexar County 1876, organized 1882, named for jurist-soldier Stockton P. Donley. County seat Clarendon; other towns include Hedley, Howardwick and Lelia Lake. Bounded by Armstrong, Carson, Gray, Wheeler, Collingsworth, Hall and Briscoe Counties.

ATHENS OF THE PANHANDLE. A History of Clarendon College. By Ethel Harvey. Burnet,Tx. $10.95. Ranger.

DONLEY COUNTY. Land O' Promise. By Virginia Browder. Quanah, Tx. 1975. 328p.,ill.,biblio.,index, 4to. $19.95. Ranger.

DUVAL

Created 1858 from Live Oak, Nueces and Starr Counties, organized 1876, named for Burr H. Duval, who was shot at Goliad. County seat

San Diego; other towns include Benavides, Freer and Realitos. Bounded by McMullen, Jim Wells, Live Oak, Brooks, Jim Hogg, Webb and LaSalle Counties.

BENAVIDES. The Town and Its Founder. By Arnoldo De Leon. n.p.,n.d.,ca.1980. 20p,ill.,notes,pc.Write.Duval.

THE DUKE OF DUVAL. The Life and Times of George Parr. By Dudley Lynch. Waco. 168p.,ill.,index. paper $5.95, Cloth $8.50. Ranger.

OIL, MUD AND GUTS. By Dorothy A. McCoy. Mission,1977.2d Ptg. 188p.,ill.,biblio. $15.00. Ranger.

A SOCIAL HISTORY OF MEXICAN AMERICANS IN NINETEENTH CENTURY DUVAL COUNTY. By Arnaldo De Leon. n.p.,n.d. ca. 1980. 20p.,ill.,notes,pc. Write. Duval.

EASTLAND

Created 1858 from Bosque, Coryell and Travis Counties, organized 1873, named for William Mosby Eastland, who drew the first black bean at Salado. County seat Eastland; other towns include Ranger, Cisco, Rising Star, Carbon and Desdemona. Bounded by Callahan, Stephens, Shackelford, Palo Pinto, Erath, Comanche and Brown Counties.

THE BEST DAMN TEACHER. By Lela L. Lloyd.Cisco, 1978. Has teaching experiences in Cisco. $9.95. Lloyd.

A CENTURY OF CISCO METHODISM. By L.L.Lloyd. Soon to be published. Lloyd.

CEMETERY INSCRIPTIONS OF EASTLAND COUNTY TEXAS. Compiled by S.B. Cawyer & W.I.Hudson. Three volumes. pc. $10.00 per volume. Ingmire.

ONE HUNDRED YEARS WITH GOD. Cisco Baptist Church. Cisco, 1980. $10.00. Sipe.

PRESBYTERIAN PATHWAYS. By Evelyn Bailey. Cisco. 1981. $10.00. Weeks.

WHERE THE RAILS CROSSED. Cisco,Texas. By Bill M. Roberts. Burnet,Tx. 1981. 112p.,ill. $13.50. Roberts.

ECTOR

Created 1887 from Tom Green County, organized 1891, named for Texas jurist Mathew D. Ector. County seat Odessa; other towns include Goldsmith and Notrees. Bounded by Winkler, Andrews, Midland, Upton, Crane and Ward Counties.

IT'S A MIRAGE!, IT'S A MIRACLE!, IT'S ODESSA. By Keith Elliott. Austin,ca.1975. 8p reprint of an article from Texas Parade magazine. 4to,pc.$5.00. Ranger.

INVENTORY OF COUNTY RECORDS, ECTOR COUNTY COURT-HOUSE ODESSA, TEXAS. Compiled by Carolyn Trigg. Austin,1973, 57p.,index, 4to, pc. $1.00. TSL.

EDWARDS

Created 1858 from Bexar County, organized 1883, named for colonizer Haden Edwards. County seat Rocksprings; other towns include Camp

Wood and Barksdale. Bounded by Sutton, Kimble, Kerr, Real, Uvalde, Kinney and Val Verde Counties.

No publications located.

ELLIS

Created 1849 from Navarro County,organized 1850, named for Judge Richard Ellis. County seat Waxahachie; other towns include Avalon, Ennis, Ferris, Italy, Midlothian, Palmer and Red Oak. Bounded by Tarrant, Dallas, Kaufman, Henderson, Navarro, HIll and Johnson Counties.

ELLIS COUNTY CEMETERIES . Two Volumes. $20.00ea. Ellis.

ELLIS COUNTY CENSUS RECORDS 1850. Index. $5.50. Heritage.

ELLIS COUNTY NATURALIZATION RECORDS. Waxahachie,Tx. 72p., $10.00. Ellis.

HISTORY OF ELLIS COUNTY,TEXAS. Compiled by Ellis County Historical Workshop. Ennis,Tx, 1972, 338p.,ill.,notes,index.$11.00. Ennis.

OLD NORTHWEST TEXAS. Navarro County. 1846-1860. By N.T. Samuels and B.R. Knox. Ft. Worth. Two volumes, 863p.,ill.,biblio., index. $50.00. Fort Worth.

TEXAS CENSUS 1850. Vol.15. Compiled by V.K. Carpenter. 1979. Reprint ed., pc. $10.00. Presley.

TRINITY UNIVERSITY. A Record of One Hundred Years. By Donald E. Everett. San Antonio, 1968. 276p.,$5.00. Ranger.

Periodical: SEARCHERS AND RESEARCHERS. Publication of the Ellis County Genealogical Society. $3 each. Ellis.

EL PASO

Created from Bexar County 1849, organized 1850, named for "The Pass of the North." County seat El Paso; other towns include Anthony, Canutillo, Fabens, San Elizario, Tornillo and Ysleta. Bounded by Hudspeth County on the east, Mexico on the south and west, and New Mexico on the north.

BEN DOWELL. El Paso's First Mayor. By Nancy Hamilton. El Paso, pc. $3.00. Ranger.

BIRTHS, DEATHS & MARRIAGES IN EL PASO NEWSPAPERS TO 1886. Easley,S.C. 1982. 226p.,index. $22.50. Ranger.

BORDERTOWN REVISITED. By Frank Mangan. El Paso. 160p., $4.95. Ranger.

THE CHICANOS OF EL PASO. An Assessment of Progress. El Paso, pc. $3.00. Ranger.

CONCORDIA CEMETERY RECORDS. Compiled by D.R. Diamond-Collier. El Paso, 1982. Two volumes. $70.00. Diamond.

DESERT IMMIGRANTS. The Mexicans of El Paso 1880-1920. By Mario T. Garcia. New Haven,Conn. 1981. $15.00. Yale.

DOWN WENT MCGINTY. El Paso in the Wonderful Nineties. By Conrey Bryson. El Paso, 1977. 150p.,$10.00. Ranger.

EL PASO IN PICTURES. By Frank Mangan. El Paso, 174p.,ill., 4to. $24.00. Ranger.

FORT BLISS. An Illustrated History. By Leon C. Metz. El Paso, 1981. 180p.,ill.,biblio.,index, 4to. $34.95. Ranger.

GUIDE TO EL PASO. By Winifred Dowling. El Paso. pc. $4.95 Ranger.

HENRY C. TROST. Architect of the Southwest. By L.C. Engelbrecht & June-Marie Engelbrecht. El Paso, 1980. 150p.,ill. $27.50. El Paso.

IMAGES/PASO DEL NORTE. By Bill Rakocy. El Paso. ill.$15.95 Ranger.

AN INTRODUCTION TO EL PASO'S SCENIC AND HISTORIC LANDMARKS. By Charles Binion. El Paso, 1970. 61p.,ill. 4to. pc. $3.50. Ranger.

JOSEPHINE CLARDY FOX. Traveler, Opera-Goer, Collector of Art, Benefactor. By Ruby Burns. El Paso. 1973. 143p., $8.00. Ranger.

LETTERS OF ERNST KOHLBERG 1875-1877. Translated by W.L. Kohlberg. El Paso, 1973. 73p.,ill.,references. paper $3.00, cloth $10.00 Ranger.

LORD BERESFORD AND LADY FLO. By Eugene O. Porter. El Paso. 1970. 44p.,ill.,biblio. pc. $3.00, cloth, $10.00. Ranger.

MOMENTS IN TIME. A History of the Tornillo Community and Its People. By Frances Segulia. $29.50. Cayote.

MUSIC IN EL PASO. 1919-1939. By R.M. Stevenson.El Paso.pc. $3.00. Ranger.

PASS OF THE NORTH. Vol.I 1519-1917. By C.L. Sonnichsen. El Paso, 1980. 472p.,ill.,biblio.,index. $20. Ranger.

PASS OF THE NORTH. Vol. II 1918-1980. By C.L. Sonnichsen. El Paso, 1980. 148p.,ill.,biblio.,index. $15.00. Ranger.

POSTWAR READJUSTMENT IN EL PASO 1945-1950. By Patricia Reschenthaler. El Paso. $3.00. Ranger.

SAN ELIZARIO. A History. By Eugene O. Porter. Austin, 1973 86p.,ill.,biblio.,index. $14.95. Ranger.

THE SCHWARTZ FAMILY OF EL PASO. By Floyd S. Fierman. El Paso, pc. $4.00 , cloth $10.00. Ranger.

SIX WHO CAME TO EL PASO. Pioneers of the 1840's. By Rex W. Strickland. El Paso, 1963. 48p.,ill.,biblio.,pc. $3.00. Ranger.

Periodical: PASSWORD. Quarterly of the El Paso County Historical Society. $15/Year with membership. Password.

ERATH

Created and organized 1856 from Bosque and Coryell Counties, named for soldier-politician George Bernard Erath. County seat Stephenville; other towns include Bluffdale and Dublin. Bounded by Palo Pinto, Hood, Somervell, Bosque, Hamilton, Comanche and Eastland Counties.

CENTENNIAL CLAIRETTE 1880-1980. By Becky Farrar. Dublin, 1980. 2d Ptg. 1982. 333p.,ill., 4to. $20.00. Green.

ERATH COUNTY CEMETERY RECORDS. $10.00. Cawyer.

ERATH COUNTY, TEXAS MARRIAGES. Compiled by Erath County Genealogical Society. Vol. I 1869-1891. Vol. 2 1891-1900. 4to.pc. $10.00 each vol. Hudson.

ERATH COUNTY, TEXAS CENSUS RECORDS 1860-1870. Compiled by W.I. Hudson & Shirley Cawyer. 104p.,4to,pc.$10.00. Cawyer.

FALLS

Created and organized 1850 from Limestone and Milam Counties, named for falls on Brazos River. County seat Marlin; other towns include Lott, Rosebud and Westphalia. Bounded by McLennan, Limestone, Bell, Milam, and Robertson Counties.

THE MARLIN COMPOUND. Letters of a Singular Family. Ed. by Frank C. Oltorf. Austin, 1968. 306p., index. $15.00. Ranger.

MARLIN COUNTY HISTORY. By W.S. Frost. Quanah, 1975. Reprint of 1909 ed. 32p., 4to. $6.00. Ranger.

FANNIN

Created 1837 from Red River County, organized 1838, named for James Walker Fannin. County seat Bonham; other towns include Bailey, Dodd City, Honey Grove and Leonard. Bounded by Lamar, Delta, Hunt, Collin and Grayson Counties, and by Oklahoma on the north.

BELOW THE LLANO ESTACADO-AND BEYOND. By Robert Hammock. Write. Fannin.

BONHAM. The Era Has Gone - But Memories Linger On. By Mrs. Lucille Hackley. Bonham, 1979. 118p., ill. Write. Fannin.

FANNIN COUNTY CENSUS RECORDS 1850. Index. $19.50. Heritage.

FANNIN COUNTY FACTS AND FOLKS. By Friends of Bonham Public Library. Dallas, 1977. 440p. Write. Fannin. •

FANNIN COUNTY, TEXAS 1850 CENSUS. Compiled by F.T. Ingmire. $9.95. Ingmire.

FANNIN COUNTY, TEXAS 1870 CENSUS. Compiled by F.T. Ingmire. $13.50. Ingmire.

FANNIN COUNTY, TEXAS CONFEDERATE PENSION APPLICATIONS. Compiled by F.T. Ingmire. $12.50. Ingmire.

FANNIN COUNTY, TEXAS LAND TITLES. Compiled by F.T. Ingmire and R.L. Thompson. St. Louis, 1979. 47p., index, 4to pc. $8.95 Ingmire.

FANNIN COUNTY, TEXAS LOG BOOK 1885-1889. Maddrey & Hunter Livery Stable. Compiled by F.T. Ingmire. $9.95. Ingmire.

FANNIN COUNTY, TEXAS MINUTES OF THE BOARD OF COMMISSIONERS. Compiled by Gifford White. $11.95. Ingmire.

FIRST SETTLERS OF FANNIN COUNTY, TEXAS. Ed. by Gifford White. $12.50. Ericson.

HISTORY OF FANNIN COUNTY, TEXAS. By. W.A. Carter. Write Fannin.

THE HISTORY OF LEONARD, TEXAS 1880-1980. Leonard, Tx, 1981. 184p., ill., $10.00. Leonard.

MARRIAGE RECORDS OF FANNIN COUNTY, TEXAS 1838-1870. Compiled by F.T. Ingmire. St. Louis, 1978. 42p., 4to. $6.95. Ingmire.

REHOBETH. A Pioneers Church and Cemetery, Fannin County, Texas 1852-1911. Creve Coeur, Mo. 1976. 2d Ptg. 59p., index, 4to. $8.95. Ingmire.

TEXAS CENSUS 1850. Vol. 16. Compiled by V.K. Carpenter. 1979. Reprint ed. pc. $10.00. Presley.

FAYETTE

Created 1837 from Bastrop and Colorado Counties organized 1838, named for the Marquis de Lafayette. County seat LaGrange; other towns include Fayetteville, Flatonia, Muldoon, Round Top, West Point, and Schulenberg. Bounded by Bastrop, Lee, Washington, Austin, Lavaca, Gonzales and Caldwell Counties.

AUSTIN COLONY PIONEERS. Including History of Bastrop, Fayette, Grimes, Montgomery and Washington Counties. By Worth S. Ray. Austin, 1970. Reprint of 1949 ed. 378p.,ill.,index. $17.50. Ranger.

AN EARLY HISTORY OF FAYETTE COUNTY. By Leonie Weyand and Houston Wade. Burnet, 1977. Reprint of 1932 ed. 383p.,ill.,index, $14.00. Ranger.

FAYETTE COUNTY. Her History and Her People. By F. Lotto. Burnet, 1978. Reprint of 1902 ed. 424p.,ill. $14.00. Ranger.

FAYETTE COUNTY. Past and Present. Edited by Marjorie Williams. LaGrange, 1976. 479p.,index. $15.00. LaGrange.

FAYETTE COUNTY CENSUS RECORDS 1850. Index.$16.00.Heritage.

FAYETTE COUNTY, TEXAS MARRIAGE RECORDS 1838-1870. Compiled by F.T. Ingmire. $10.95. Ingmire.

INVENTORY OF COUNTY RECORDS FAYETTE COUNTY COURTHOUSE LA GRANGE, TEXAS. Compiled by Maurice Fortin, et al. Denton, 1979. Two volumes. 197,181pp.,map,index,4to.pc.$2.00 for both. TSL.

SCHULENBERG. 100 Years on the Road with Brief Histories of Old Lyons and High Hill. By Jane Knapik. Quanah,1973. 2d Ptg. 229p. ill.,index. $11.00. Ranger.

TEXAS CENSUS 1850. Vol. 6. Compiled by V.K. Carpenter. 1979. Reprint ed. pc. $10.00. Presley.

FISHER

Created 1876 from Bexar County, organized 1886, named for Texas Revolutionist Samuel Rhoads Fisher. County seat Roby; other towns include Hamlin and Rotan. Bounded by Kent, Stonewall, Jones, Nolan, Taylor, Mitchell and Scurry Counties.

No publications located.

FLOYD

Created 1876 from Bexar County, organized 1890, named for Dolphin W. Floyd, one of the "thirty-two from Gonzales." County seat Floydada; other towns include Lockney, Lone Star and South Plains. Bounded by Swisher, Briscoe, Motley, Dickens, Crosby, Lubbock and Hale Counties.

THE EARLY HISTORY OF FLOYD COUNTY. Canyon, 1947. 147p. ill.,biblio.,index. paper $10.00, cloth $14.00. Panhandle.

THE HISTORY OF FLOYD COUNTY, 1876-1979. $37.50. Floyd.

FOARD

Created and organized 1891 from Cottle, Hardeman, King and Knox

Counties, named for Confederate Major Robert J. Foard. County seat Crowell; other towns include Thalia. Bounded by Cottle, Hardeman, Knox, Wilbarger, Baylor and King Counties.

THEY LOVED THE LAND. Foard County History. By Bailey Phelps. Burnet, Tx. 1969. 2d Ptg., 399p., ill., 4to., $25.00. Ranger.

FORT BEND

Created 1837 from Austin County, organized 1838, named for pioneer blockhouse Fort Bend. County seat Richmond; other towns include Needville, Sugar Land, Rosenberg and Katy. Bounded by Austin, Waller, Harris, Brazoria and Wharton Counties.

FORT BEND COUNTY CENSUS 1850. Index. $6.00. Heritage.

FORT BEND COUNTY SESQUICENTENNIAL 1822-1972. 1972. 72p. pc. $3.00. Fort Bend.

HISTORIC, ROMANTIC RICHMOND 1822-1982. By Roberta Christensen. Burnet, 1982. 175p., ill., index, 4to. $25.00. Ranger.

HISTORY OF FORT BEND COUNTY. By A.J. Sowell. Reprint of 1904 ed. $15.00. Fort Bend.

HISTORY OF FORT BEND COUNTY. By Clarence R. Wharton. San Antonio, 1939. Reprint ed. $15.00. Fort Bend.

THE JAY BIRDS OF FORT BEND COUNTY. By Pauline Yelderman. Waco, 1979. $17.00. Fort Bend.

Periodical: AROUND THE BEND. Quarterly of the Fort Bend County Genealogical Society. Write. FBGS.

FRANKLIN

Created and organized 1875 from Titus County, named probably for Judge Benjamin C. Franklin. County seat Mount Vernon; other towns include Winnsboro. Bounded by Lamar, Delta, Red River, Titus, Camp, Wood and Hopkins Counties.

No Publications Located.

FREESTONE

Created 1850 from Limestone County, organized 1851, named for native stone. County seat Fairfield; other towns include Kirvin, Streetman, Teague and Wortham. Bounded by Navarro, Henderson, Anderson, Leon and Limestone Counties.

THE FAIRFIELD CONFEDERATE REUNIONS 1890-1933. By P.D. Browne, pc. $1.00. BRI.

HISTORY OF FREESTONE COUNTY, TEXAS. By the Freestone County Historical Commission. 1978. $35.00. Freestone.

OFFICIAL TEXAS HISTORICAL MARKERS OF FREESTONE COUNTY. 1974. pc. $3.00. BRI

FRIO

Created and organized in 1871 from Atascosa, Bexar and Uvalde Counties.

Named for Frio ("cold") River. County seat Pearsall; other towns include Dilley and Moore. Bounded by Uvalde, Medina, Atascosa, McMullen, La Salle, Dimmit, and Zavala Counties.

HISTORIC FRIO COUNTY 1871-1971. Pearsall,Tx., 1971. 80 unn. pages, ill.,4to.pc.$5.00. Frio.

GAINES

Created 1876 from Bexar County, organized 1905, named for James Gaines, who helped draft and signed the Texas Declaration of Independence. County seat Seminole; other towns include Higginbotham and Seagraves. Bounded by Yoakum, Terry, Dawson, Martin and Andrews Counties, and by New Mexico on the west.

THE GAINES COUNTY STORY. A History of Gaines County,Texas. Edited by Margaret Coward. Seagraves,Tx. 1974. 536p.,ill.,index, 4to. $12.50. Ranger.

GALVESTON

Created 1838 from Brazoria County, organized 1839, named for Count Bernardo de Galvez. County seat Galveston; other towns include Arcadia, Alta Loma, Bacliff, Clear Lake Shores, Dickinson, Hitchcock, Friendswood, Kemah, La Marque, Port Bolivar, League City and Texas City. Bounded by Chambers, Harris and Brazoria Counties and by the Gulf of Mexico.

DICKINSON. Taller Than the Pines. By Jim Hudson. Burnet, 1979. 139p.,ill.,biblio.,index. $10.00. Ranger.

BAPTISMAL RECORDS OF ST. JOSEPH CATHOLIC CHURCH-GALVESTON,TEXAS 1860-1900. Compiled by Galveston County Genealogical Society. 212p., 4to.,pc. $10.50. Sheffield.

GALVESTON COUNTY CENSUS RECORDS 1850. Index. $23.00. Heritage.

GALVESTON COUNTY TOMBSTONE INSCRIPTIONS VOL.I. Compiled by Texas City Ancestry Searchers. index, 4to. $5.50. Sheffield.

THE GALVESTON ERA. The Texas Crescent on the Eve of Secession. By Earl Wesley Fornell. Austin, 1961. 1976 reissue. 355p.,ill. biblio.,index, pc. $10.00. Ranger.

INVENTORY OF COUNTY RECORDS GALVESTON COUNTY COURTHOUSE GALVESTON,TEXAS. Compiled by Diane Hill,et al. Denton, 1980, Three volumes. 205,185,185 pp., map, 4to,pc. $9 for 3 vols. TSL.

JULIUS STOCKFLETH. Gulf Coast Marine and Landscape Painter. By James P. McGuire. San Antonio, 1976. 161p.,ill. 4to. $10.00. Ranger.

RECORD OF INTERMENTS OF THE CITY OF GALVESTON. Compiled by Mrs. Peggy H. Gregory. Covers period 1859-1872. Houston, 1976. 242p.,index,4to, pc. $11.00. Gregory.

SEARCHER'S TALES OF THE TEXAS CITY ANCESTRY SEARCHERS. By Texas City Ancestry Searchers. 1978. 168p.,index,4to.pc. Vol.1 $6.00. Vol. 2 $6.00. Sheffield.

TEXAS CENSUS 1850. Vol. 3. Compiled by V.K. Carpenter. 1979. Reprint ed. pc. $10.00. Presley.

TEXAS HEROES BURIED ON GALVESTON ISLAND. By Sidney Sherman Chapter D.A.R. of Texas. Easley,S.C. 1982. 88p., index. $10.00. Ranger.

THE UNIVERSITY OF TEXAS MEDICAL BRANCH AT GALVESTON. A Seventy-five Year History. By Medical Branch of the University of Texas. Austin, 1967. 457p.,ill. $22.50. Ranger.

A WEEKEND IN SEPTEMBER. By John Edward Weems. College Station,Tx. 1980. Reprint ed. 192p.,ill. $11.00. Ranger.

GARZA

Created 1876 from Bexar County, organized 1907, named for pioneer family. County seat Post; other towns include Southland. Bounded by Lynn, Lubbock, Crosby, Dickens, Kent, Scurry and Borden Counties.

THE ESPUELA LAND AND CATTLE COMPANY. By W.C. Holden. Austin, 1970. 268p.,ill.,biblio.,index, $9.00. Ranger.

WAGON WHEELS. A History of Garza County. Edited by Charles Didway. Burnet, 1980. 2d Ptg.,340p.,ill. 4to. $25.00. Ranger.

GILLESPIE

Created and organized 1848 from Bexar and Travis Counties, named for Ranger Richard A. Gillespie, who was killed in the War with Mexico. County seat Fredericksburg; other towns include Harper and Stonewall. Bounded by Mason, Llano, Blanco, Kendall, Kerr and Kimble Counties.

FREDERICKSBURG,TEXAS. The First Fifty Years. Translated by C.L. Wissman. Fredericksburg, 1971. Originally published in German in 1896. $6.95. Fredericksburg.

GILLESPIE COUNTY CENSUS RECORDS 1850. Index. $8.00 Heritage.

HISTORICAL HOMES IN AND AROUND FREDERICKSBURG. By Elise Kowert. Fredericksburg, 1980. 206p.,ill. $12.00. Fredericksburg.

KIRCHEN-BUCH. Church Record Book of the Vereins-Kirche 1849-1870. Translated by Ella Gold. Fredericksburg, 1981. Write. Gillespie.

OLD HOMES AND BUILDINGS OF FREDERICKSBURG. By Elise Kowert. Fredericksburg, 1981. lst pub. in 1977. 216p., $12.00. Fredericksburg.

PIONEERS IN GOD'S HILLS. A History of Fredericksburg and Gillespie County People and Events. Fredericksburg. Vol.I, 1960. Vol. II, 1974. $11.00/volume. Gillespie.

TEXAS CENSUS 1850. Vol. 8. Compiled by V.K. Carpenter. 1979. Reprint Ed. pc. $10.00. Presley.

GLASSCOCK

Created 1887 from Tom Green County, organized 1893, named for pioneer George Washington Glasscock. County seat Garden City. Bounded by Martin, Howard, Sterling, Reagan, Upton and Midland Counties.

INVENTORY OF COUNTY RECORDS GLASSCOCK COUNTY COURTHOUSE GARDEN CITY, TEXAS. Compiled by Maurice G. Fortin, et al. Austin, 1977. 121p., map, index, 4to, pc, $1.00. TSL

GOLIAD

One of the original Texas counties. Created 1836, organized in 1837, name is probably an anagram of (H)idalgo. County seat Goliad; other towns include Schroeder and Weesatche. Bounded by Karnes, DeWitt, Victoria, Refugio and Bee Counties.

GOLIAD COUNTY CENSUS RECORDS 1850. Index. $4.50.Heritage.

GOLIAD COUNTY MARRIAGE RECORDS 1870-1890. Compiled by F.T. Ingmire. St. Louis, 1981. 26p.,index, 4to.,pc. $9.50. Ingmire.

HISTORY OF GOLIAD. By E.B. Cole and J.L. Pruett. Due for publication in 1983. Write. Goliad.

INVENTORY OF COUNTY RECORDS GOLIAD COUNTY COURTHOUSE GOLIAD, TEXAS. Compiled by James E. Riney, et al. Denton, 1980. 189p., map, index. 4to. pc. $3.00. TSL.

REMEMBER GOLIAD! By Clarence Wharton. Houston, 1931. Reprint ed. of 1968 with added introduction, photographs and index. 104p., ill.,folding map, index. $15.00. Ranger.

GONZALES

One of the original Texas counties. Created 1836, organized in 1837, named for Rafael Gonzales, one-time governor of Coahuila and Texas. County seat Gonzales; other towns include Harwood, Smiley, Waelder and Nixon. Bounded by Guadalupe,Caldwell,Bastrop,Fayette, Wilson, DeWitt and Karnes Counties.

GONZALES. "The Lexington of Texas." By Gonzales Art Group. Gonzales. 2d Ed. 40 unn. pages, ill. 4to, pc. $2.00. Gonzales Museum.

GONZALES COUNTY CENSUS RECORDS 1850. Index. $11.00. Heritage.

RX TAKE ONE CANNON. The Gonzales Come & Take It Cannon of October, 1835. Shiner, 1981. 150p., ill.,biblio.,pc.$6.00. Ranger.

THE TIES THAT BIND. By Marjorie Hyatt. $22.00. Hyatt.

Publication: YESTERDAYS. Publication of the South Texas Genealogical and Historical Society. $8.00 per year. Gonzales.

GRAY

Created 1876 from Bexar County, organized 1902, named for politician-soldier Peter W. Gray. County seat Pampa; other towns include Lefors and McLean. Bounded by Roberts, Hemphill, Wheeler, Collingsworth, Donley, Armstrong, Carson and Hutchinson Counties.

BLUE BOOK OF THE TEXAS PANHANDLE. Ed. by David Harris. Pampa, Tx. $35.00. Pampa.

FOR THE REASON WE CLIMB MOUNTAINS...Gray County 1902-1982. By E. Nolte. Pampa,Tx. 1982, 35p.,ill.,biblio.,4to.,pc.$3.00.Thelma.

HISTORY OF POST OFFICE. Pampa,Texas 1892-1982. By Ivo Denson. Pampa,Tx 1982. 16 unn. pages. pc. $1.00. Thelma.

GRAYSON

Created and organized 1846 from Fannin County; named for early Texan Peter William Grayson. County seat Sherman; other towns include Howe, Van Alstyne, Whitesboro and Whitewright. Bounded by Fannin, Collin, Denton and Cooke County, and by Oklahoma on the north.

ANCESTORS AND DESCENDANTS OF GRAYSON COUNTY, TEXAS. Sherman, 1980, 688p, ill.,index. $35.00. GCGS.

GRAYSON COUNTY CENSUS RECORDS 1850. Index. $10.50 Heritage.

HISTORY OF GRAYSON COUNTY, TEXAS. Vol. 1 $36.75. Vol. 2. $49.50. Grayson.

I REMEMBER THINGS. An Informal History of Tioga, Texas. By Ross Estes. Quanah, 1977. 130p.,ill.,index. $8.00. Ranger.

LOST SHERMAN. $12.00. Sherman.

MARRIAGE RECORDS OF GRAYSON COUNTY, TEXAS 1846-1877. Compiled by F.T. Ingmire. St. Louis, 1979. 79p.,index, 4to. $8.95. Ingmire.

TEXAS CENSUS 1850. Vol. 16. Compiled by V.K. Carpenter. 1979. Reprint ed. pc. $10.00. Presley.

GREGG

Created and organized 1873 from Rusk and Upshur Counties, named for Confederate General John Gregg. County seat Longview; other towns include Gladewater, Spring Hill, Kilgore and White Oak. Bounded by Smith, Upshur, Harrison and Rusk Counties.

BOOM TOWN. Kilgore, Texas. By Al Eason. Kilgore,Tx, 144p. ill., paper $8.00, cloth $11.00. Kilgore.

GLADEWATER CENTENNIAL BOOK. By Centennial Committee. Gladewater,Tx. 1973. $10.00. Gladewater.

GLADEWATER HISTORY. 1976. $10.00. Gladewater.

GREGG COUNTY TEXAS MARRIAGE LICENSE INDEX. Books A,B,C and D 1873-1895. Compiled by Nancy B. Ruff. 120p. 4to.,paper. $12.50. Ruff.

LONGVIEW, TEXAS CENTENNIAL 1870-1970. By Centennial Book Committee. Longview, 1970. 76p.,ill. 4to.,pc. $3.00. Longview.

GRIMES

Created and organized 1846 from Montgomery County, named probably for early settler Jesse Grimes. County seat Anderson; other towns include Bedias and Navasota. Bounded by Brazos, Madison, Walker, Montgomery, Waller and Washington Counties.

AUSTIN COLONY PIONEERS. Including History of Bastrop, Fayette, Grimes, Montgomery and Washington Counties. By Worth S. Ray. Austin, 1970. Reprint of 1949 ed. 378p.,ill.,index. $17.50. Ranger.

GRIMES COUNTY CENSUS RECORDS 1850. Index. $13.50.Heritage.

HISTORY OF GRIMES COUNTY. By Grimes County Historical Commission. 1982. 759p., Write. Grimes.

NORTHERN GRIMES COUNTY CEMETERIES. Compiled by The Generation Gap. In preparation. Write. Madison.

TEXAS CENSUS 1850. Vol. 5. Compiled by V.K. Carpenter. 1979. Reprint ed., pc. $10.00. Presley.

GUADALUPE

Created and organized 1846 from Bexar and Gonzales Counties, named for Guadalupe River. County seat Seguin; other towns include Cibolo, McQueeney and Schertz. Bounded by Bexar, Comal, Caldwell, Gonzales and Wilson Counties.

AN AUTHENTIC HISTORY OF GUADALUPE COUNTY. By Willie Mae Weinert. Seguin, 1951. Reprint ed. 96p., ill., index. pc. $5.00 Guadalupe.

GUADALUPE COUNTY CENSUS RECORDS 1850. Index. $7.00 Heritage.

INVENTORY OF COUNTY RECORDS GUADALUPE COUNTY COURTHOUSE SEGUIN, TEXAS. Compiled by Paul H. Carlson. Denton, 1979. 265p., map, 4to., pc. $1.00. TSL.

TEXAS CENSUS 1850. Vol. 7. Compiled by V.K. Carpenter. 1979. Reprint ed., pc. $10.00. Presley.

HALE

Created from Bexar County 1876, organized 1888, named for Lt. John C. Hale, killed at San Jacinto. County seat Plainview; other towns include Edmonson, Abernathy, Hale Center, Petersburg, Cotton Center and Seth Ward. Bounded by Lamb, Castro, Swisher, Floyd, Lubbock, Crosby and Hockley Counties.

HALE COUNTY FACTS AND FOLKLORE. Ed. by Vera Dean Wofford. Lubbock, 1978. 787p., ill., index, 4to. $18.00. Ranger.

INVENTORY OF COUNTY RECORDS HALE COUNTY COURTHOUSE PLAINVIEW, TEXAS. Denton, 1979. 265p., map, index, 4to. pc. $1.00. TSL.

PLAINVIEW. A Pictorial History. Vol. I 1887-1912. Compiled by C. Gwin Morris. Plainview, Tx. 1971. 39p., ill, notes, pc. $4.00. Harrison.

Publication: HALE COUNTY HISTORY. Quarterly of the Hale County Historical Commission. $10/Year or $3.00 per copy. Hale.

HALL

Created 1876 from Bexar and Young Counties, organized 1890, named for Texas colonist Warren D.C. Hall. County seat Memphis; other towns include Estelline, Lakeview and Turkey. Bounded by Donley, Collingsworth, Childress, Cottle, Motley and Briscoe Counties.

HALL COUNTY HERITAGE. By Virginia Browder. Canyon, Tx. In preparation. Staked Plains.

LEGEND OF A COUNTRY DOCTOR. A History of Turkey, Texas. By Pauline Gilmore. Quanah, 1978. 104p., ill. $8.00. Ranger.

HAMILTON

Created and organized 1858 from Bosque, Comanche and Lampasas Counties, named for Texas diplomat James Hamilton. County seat Hamilton; other towns include Hico and Evant. Bounded by Comanche, Erath, Bosque, Coryell, Lampasas and Mills Counties.

No Publications Located.

HANSFORD

Created 1876 from Bexar and Young counties, organized 1889, named for physician-jurist John M. Hansford. County seat Spearman; other towns include Morse and Gruver. Bounded by Sherman, Moore, Roberts, Hutchinson and Ochiltree Counties, and by Oklahoma on the north.

HANSFORD COUNTY HISTORY II. 1982. $46.20. Robertson.

HARDEMAN

Created from Fannin County 1858, re-created 1876, organized 1884, named for brothers Bailey and Thomas Jones Hardeman. County seat Quanah; other towns include Chillicothe and Goodlett. Bounded by Childress, Cottle, King, Foard and Wilbarger Counties, and by Oklahoma on the north.

HARDEMAN COUNTY. Agricultural and Industrial Edition. Ed. by Harry Koch. Quanah, 1972. Reprint of 1920 ed. 92p.,ill.,folio, pc. $10.00. Ranger.

THE LAST FRONTIER. The Story of Hardeman County. By Bill Neal. Quanah, 1966. 286p.,$25.00. Ranger.

HARDIN

Created and organized from Jefferson and Liberty Counties 1858, named for pioneer William Hardin. County seat Kountze; other towns include Lumberton, Sour Lake, Honey Island, Silsbee and Saratoga. Bounded by Tyler, Polk, Liberty, Jefferson, Orange and Jasper Counties.

BIG THICKET LEGACY. Compiled by Campbell Loughmiller. Austin, 1977. 224p.,ill.,pc. $8.95. Ranger.

HARDIN COUNTY CEMETERIES. Compiled by Mrs. Mildred S. Wright. $15.50. Southeast.

HARDIN COUNTY, TEXAS MARRIAGES 1858-1900. $7.50. Southeast.

HARRIS

Created 1836, organized 1837, name shortened from Harrisburg, which was named for early settler John Richardson Harris. County seat is Houston; other towns include Pasadena, Bellaire, LaPorte, Baytown, Deer Park, Humble, and more. Bounded byChambers, Liberty,Fort Bend, Waller, Montgomery, Brazoria and Galveston Counties.

GERMAN COLONISTS IN HOUSTON. By Dorothy E. Justman. Burnet, 384p.,ill,biblio.,index, 4to. $16.00. Ranger.

HARRIS COUNTY CENSUS RECORDS 1850. Index.$23.00.Heritage.

HARRIS COUNTY NATURALIZATION INTENT RECORDS. $3.00. Chaparral.

HOUSTON. A History. By David G. McComb. Austin, 1981. 325p. ill. paper, $8.95, cloth $25.00. Ranger.

HOUSTON. A Historical Portrait. By John L. Davis. Austin, 233p.,ill.4to. $25.00. Ranger.

HOUSTON BY STAGES. A History of the Theatre in Houston. By Sue Dauphin. Burnet, 500p.,ill.,index. $25.00. Ranger.

THE HOUSTON SYMPHONY ORCHESTRA 1913-1971. By Hubert Roussel. Austin, 1972. 257p.,$12.50. Ranger.

THE INDUSTRIAL ADVANTAGES OF HOUSTON,TEXAS AND ENVIRONS. Also a Series of Sketches of the City's Representative Business Enterprises. Houston, 1894. Reprint of 1977. 138p.,ill., index, pc. $8.50. Ranger.

MARRIAGE RECORDS HARRIS COUNTY, TEXAS VOL. I 1837-1865. Vol. A-D of Harris County Records. Compiled by Marie Russell. $15.00. Russell.

A NIGHT OF VIOLENCE. The Houston Riot of 1917. Baton Rouge, La., 1976. 338p.,maps, sources,index. $16.95. LSU.

THE PORT OF HOUSTON. A History. By Marilyn M. Sibley. Austin, 1968. 262p.,ill.,biblio.,index. $15.00. Ranger.

TEXAS CENSUS 1850. Vol. 10. Compiled by V.K. Carpenter. 1979. Reprint ed. pc. $10.00. Presley.

WHERE'S HOUSTON? By Keith Elliott. Offset reprint of article in Texas Parade magazine. Austin,ca.1968, 16p.,pc. $5.00. Ranger.

Periodical: THE GENEALOGICAL RECORD. Quarterly of Houston Genealogical Forum. $7.50/Year. Forum.

Periodical: THE HOUSTON REVIEW. History and Culture of the Gulf Coast. Published 3 times a year. $7.50/Year Individuals; $12.00 for Institutions. HR.

Periodical: THE LIVING TREE NEWS. Quarterly of the Harris County Genealogical Society. $8/Year. LTN.

Periodical: THE ROADRUNNER. Publication of the Chaparral Genealogical Society. Write. Chaparral.

HARRISON

Created 1839 from Shelby County, organized 1842, named for Texas Revolutionist Jonas Harrison. County seat Marshall; other towns include Hallsville, Uncertain, Karnack and Waskom. Bounded by Marion, Upshur, Gregg, Rusk and Panola Counties, and by Louisiana on the east.

HARRISON COUNTY CENSUS RECORDS 1850. Index. $32.50. Heritage.

INVENTORY OF COUNTY RECORDS HARRISON COUNTY COURTHOUSE MARSHALL, TEXAS. Compiled by Seth Wilson. Denton, 1979. 297p.,map,index,4to, pc. $2.00. TSL.

LAND CERTIFICATES FROM SHELBY AND HARRISON COUNTIES, TEXAS 1838-1840. Compiled by Gifford White. pc. $12.50. Ingmire.

MAURICE BARRYMORE AND THE INCIDENT AT MARSHALL. By C. Richard King. Marshall,Tx. Offset reprint from 1963 article in East Texas Historical Journal. 15p.,notes, pc. $2.50. Harrison.

THE MILITARY OCCUPATION OF MARSHALL,TEXAS by the 8th Illinois Volunteer Infantry U.S.A. 1865. By Max Lale. Marshall,Tx. Offset reprint from periodical. 8p.,notes, pc. $2.50. Harrison.

MISSOURI'S CONFEDERATE CAPITAL IN MARSHALL, TEXAS. By William Geise. Marshall,Tx. Offset reprint from periodical, 1962. 15p.,notes, pc. $2.50. Harrison.

TEXAS CENSUS 1850. Vol. 19. Compiled by V.K. Carpenter. 1979. Reprint ed. pc. $10.00. Presley.

HARTLEY

Created 1876 from Bexar and Young Districts, organized 1891, named for pioneers O.C. and R.K. Hartley. County seat Channing; other towns include Hartley and part of Dalhart. Bounded by Dallam,Moore, Potter and Oldham Counties, and by New Mexico on the west.

THE BOOK OF YEARS. A History of Dallam and Hartley Counties. By Lillie Mae Hunter. Hereford,Tx. 1969. 206p., ill.,index. $12.50. Ranger.

HASKELL

Created 1858 from Milam and Fannin Counties, recreated 1876, organized 1885, named for Goliad Massacre victim Charles R. Haskell. County seat Haskell; other towns include Sagerton, Rochester, Rule, Stamford, and Weinert. Bounded by Stonewall, King, Knox, Baylor, Throckmorton, Shackelford and Jones Counties.

HASKELL COUNTY AND ITS PIONEERS. By Rex A. Felker. Quanah,Tx. 1975. 323p.,ill. 4to. $20.00. Ranger.

HAYS

Created from Travis County and organized 1843, named for Texas Ranger Captain John Coffee Hays. County seat San Marcos; other towns are Buda, Dripping Springs,Kyle and Wimberley. Bounded by Blanco, Travis, Caldwell, Guadalupe and Comal Counties.

HAYS COUNTY CENSUS RECORDS 1850. Index. $4.50. Heritage.

HISTORICAL MARKERS IN HAYS COUNTY 1907-1976. By Tula Townsend Wyatt. Write. Wyatt.

THE PRAIRIE CITY. A History of Kyle, Texas 1880-1980. Burnet, 1981. 481p.,ill.,index. $25.00. Ranger.

TEXAS CENSUS 1850. Vol. 8. Compiled by V.K. Carpenter. 1979. Reprint ed. pc. $10.00. Presley.

HEMPHILL

Created 1876 from Bexar and Young Districts, organized 1887, named for soldier-jurist John Hemphill. County seat Canadian. Bounded by Wheeler,Gray,Roberts, Ochiltree and Lipscomb Counties, and by Oklahoma on the north.

COWMEN AND LADIES. History of Hemphill County. By Sallie Harris. $18.38. Harris.

HEMPHILL COUNTY MARRIAGE RECORDS. Write. Hemphill.

HENDERSON

Created and organized 1846 from Houston and Nacogdoches Counties, named for James Pinckney Henderson, first governor of the State of Texas. County seat Athens; other towns include Murchison, Malakoff, Brownsboro and Trinidad. Bounded by Ellis, Kaufman, Van Zandt, Smith, Cherokee, Anderson, Freestone and Navarro Counties.

ATHENS REVIEW. Reprint of 1901 newspaper. $1.50. Henderson.

FAMILY HISTORIES OF HENDERSON COUNTY, TEXAS. 1981. 320p., ill., index. $45.00. Henderson.

HENDERSON COUNTY CENSUS RECORDS 1850. Index. $7.00 Heritage.

HENDERSON COUNTY MARRIAGE RECORDS. Vol. 2. Projected for 1983 publication. Write. Henderson.

OLD HOMES OF HENDERSON COUNTY. 1982. ill., index. $35.00 Henderson.

SOUTHLAND. Reprint of 1904 newspaper. $1.50. Henderson.

TEXAS CENSUS 1850. Vol. 14. Compiled by V.K. Carpenter. 1979. Reprint ed. pc. $10.00. Presley.

Periodical: TEXAS A.G.O. Quarterly of the Athens Genealogical Organization. $10/Year with membership. Athens.

HIDALGO

Created and organized 1852 from Cameron and Starr Counties; named for Mexican priest and patriot Miguel Hidalgo y Costilla. County seat Edinburg; other towns include Alamo, Ed Couch, Donna, McAllen, Mission, Mercedes, Pharr, San Juan and Weslaco. Bounded by Starr, Cameron, Willacy, Kenedy, Brooks Counties, and by Mexico on the south.

EDINBURG. A Story of a Town. Edited by Harry Quin. 1977. $7.88. Hidalgo.

INVENTORY OF COUNTY RECORDS HIDALGO COUNTY COURTHOUSE EDINBURG, TEXAS. Compiled by Lillian Noyes, et al. Denton, 1979. Two volumes. 249,187pp., map, index, 4to, pc. $2.00 both. TSL.

MCALLEN. So Near and Yet So Foreign. By Keith Elliott. Offset reprint from Texas Parade magazine. Austin, ca. 1968. 8p., pc. $5.00 Ranger.

WESLACO 1919-1969. Official Historical Booklet. By Eleanor Mortenson, ed. Weslaco, Tx. 1969. 100p., ill. 4to., pc. $3.00. Weslaco.

HILL

Created and organized 1853 from Navarro County, named for pioneer Doctor George W. Hill. County seat Hillsboro; other towns include Hubbard, Itasca, Malone, Whitney and Aquilla. Bounded by Johnson, Bosque, Ellis, Navarro, Limestone and McLennan Counties.

ABBOTT, TEXAS' FIRST 100 YEARS. By Odette Bottom. 130p. $11.00. Bottom.

HISTORY OF HILL COUNTY. 1980. 500p., $17.50. Hill.

HILL COUNTY, TEXAS MARRIAGE RECORDS 1873-1880. Compiled by F.T. Ingmire. $7.95. Ingmire.

OLD NORTHWEST TEXAS. Navarro County 1846-1860. By N.T. Samuels and B.R. Knox. Ft. Worth. Two volumes, 863p., ill., biblio., index. $50.00. Fort Worth.

HOCKLEY

Created 1876 from Bexar and Young Districts, organized 1921, named for Texas Revolutionary soldier George W. Hockley. County seat Levelland; other towns include Anton, Whitharral, Ropesville, Smyer and Sundown. Bounded by Cochran, Lamb, Hale, Lubbock, Lynn, Terry, Bailey and Yoakum Counties.

HISTORY OF HOCKLEY COUNTY. The First Fifty Years 1921-1971. Canyon, Tx. 1978. $17.50. Brasher.

LEVELLAND. 86p. $7.50. Levelland.

HOOD

Created and organized 1866 from Johnson County, named for Confederate General John Bell Hood. County seat Granbury; other towns include Thorp Springs, Lipan and Tolar. Bounded by Palo Pinto, Parker, Johnson, Somervell and Erath Counties.

HOOD COUNTY IN PICTURE AND STORY. By Granbury Junior Woman's Club. Granbury, Tx. 1978. $15.00. Durham.

OLD NORTHWEST TEXAS. Navarro County 1846-1860. By N.T. Samuels and B.R. Knox. Ft. Worth. Two volumes, 863p., ill., biblio. index. $50.00. Fort Worth.

SCENES IN GRANBURY AND HOOD COUNTY. By J.C. Campbell Granbury,Tx. 1975. 19p.,ill.,pc. $2.25. Cammac.

THE STORY OF COMANCHE PEAK. Landmark of Hood County. Glen Rose, Tx. 1970. 69p., $5.00. Maloney.

HOPKINS

Created and organized 1846 from Lamar and Nacogdoches County, named for pioneer David Hopkins. County seat Sulphur Springs; other towns include Brashear, Sulphur Bluff, Como, Cumby and Tara. Bounded by Hunt, Delta, Wood, Franklin and Rains Counties.

EARLY HISTORY OF HOPKINS COUNTY, TEXAS. By E.B. Fleming. Wolfe City, Tx. 1902. Reprint of 1976. 183p., $12.50. Hopkins.

EARLY MARRIAGES (1844-1856) HOPKINS COUNTY, TEXAS. pc. $6.00. O'Brien.

HERITAGE FROM THE PAST. Sketches from Hopkins County History. By Celia M. Wright. Sulphur Springs, Tx. 1959. Reprint of 1981. pc. $5.50. Hopkins.

HOPKINS COUNTY CENSUS RECORDS 1850. Index. $14.50. Heritage.

MARRIAGE RECORDS OF HOPKINS COUNTY,TEXAS 1846-1880. Compiled by F.T. Ingmire. St.Louis,1980. 76p.,index,4to,pc.$8.95. Ingmire.

TEXAS CENSUS 1850 Vol. 17. Compiled by V.K. Carpenter. 1979. Reprint ed. pc. $10.00. Presley.

HOUSTON

Created and organized 1837 from Nacogdoches County, named for Sam Houston. County seat Crockett; other towns include Lovelady, Kennard and Grassland. Bounded by Anderson, Cherokee, Angelina, Trinity, Walker, Madison and Leon Counties.

HEROES AND HEROINES OF HOUSTON COUNTY. By Eliza Bishop. Grapeland,Tx. 1981. 51p.,ill.,index, 4to.,pc. $5.00. Houston.

HOUSTON COUNTY CENSUS RECORDS 1850. Index. $12.00. Heritage.

HOUSTON COUNTY IN THE CIVIL WAR. By T.N. Mainer. Crockett,Tx. 1981. 141p.,ill.,biblio.,index,pc. $10.00. Houston.

TEXAS CENSUS 1850 Vol.11. Compiled by V.K. Carpenter. 1979. Reprint ed. pc. $10.00. Presley.

HOWARD

Created from Bexar County 1876, organized 1882, named for jurist-legislator Volney E. Howard. County seat Big Spring; other towns include Forsan, Luther and Coahoma. Bounded by Martin, Glasscock, Dawson, Borden, Sterling, Mitchell and Scurry Counties.

HOWARD COUNTY HISTORY BOOK. 1882-1982. Big Spring, Tx. 1982. $55.00. HCHC.

HUDSPETH

Created and organized from El Paso County 1917, named for United States Senator Claude B. Hudspeth. County seat Sierra Blanca; other towns include Dell City, Fort Hancock and McNary. Bounded by El Paso and Culberson Counties, New Mexico on the north and Mexico on the south.

No Publications Located.

HUNT

Created and organized 1846 from Fannin and Nacogdoches Counties, named for Republic of Texas official Memucan Hunt. County seat Greenville; other towns include Caddo Mills, Commerce, Lone Oak, Quinlan and Wolfe City. Bounded by Fannin, Collin, Rockwall, Van Zandt, Kaufman, Rains, Hopkins and Delta Counties.

EARLY RECORDS OF HUNT COUNTY,TEXAS. Compiled by L.D. Story. 42p, index, 4to, pc. $6.00. Search.

HISTORICAL DOCUMENTS OF CENTRAL CHRISTIAN CHURCH GREENVILLE, HUNT COUNTY TEXAS. 100p.,folio,pc.$8.00. Search.

HONORABLE MENTION. Early Families, Hunt County,Texas. Compiled by June Applen. Quinlan,Tx. Two Volumes. 140 & 146pp. index, 4to.,pc. $15.50 each volume. Applen.

HUNT COUNTY, TEXAS ARCHIVES AND PIONEERS. Vol. I. Compiled by F.T. Ingmire. 415p.,$24.95. Ingmire.

HUNT COUNTY, TEXAS ARCHIVES AND PIONEERS, Vol. II. Record Book "A" Part I (1846-1850). Compiled by F.T. Ingmire. 249p.,index.pc. $17.95. Ingmire.

HUNT COUNTY, TEXAS ARCHIVES AND PIONEERS. Vol. III. Record Book "A" Part II (1849-1851) Compiled by F.T. Ingmire. $20.95. Ingmire.

HUNT COUNTY, TEXAS ESTRAY RECORD BOOK "A". Compiled by F.T. Ingmire. St. Louis, 1980. index, 4to. Two Parts. $17.95 ea. part. Ingmire.

HUNT COUNTY CENSUS RECORDS 1850. Index. $9.50. Heritage.

HUNT COUNTY, TEXAS 1850 CENSUS AND CONSORTS. Compiled by F.T.Ingmire. $8.95. Ingmire.

TEXAS CENSUS 1850. Vol. 16. Compiled by V.K. Carpenter. 1979. Reprint ed. pc. $10.00. Presley.

HUNT COUNTY, TEXAS CENSUS 1860. Compiled by Loraine D. Story. 144p.,index, 4to, pc. $9.50. Search.

HUNT COUNTY, TEXAS 1870 U.S.CENSUS. Compiled by F.T. Ingmire. 149p., $11.95. Ingmire.

HUNT COUNTY, TEXAS CEMETERY INSCRIPTIONS. Four volumes. $16.95 each Volumes I-3, Volume 4 is $18.95. Ingmire.

HUNT COUNTY, TEXAS JOHNNY REBS Compiled by F.T. Ingmire. $10.95. Ingmire.

HUNT COUNTY, TEXAS LOG BOOK-HARTGROVE COLLEGE FACULTY MINUTES-ARDMORE, IT, 1895 -- STUDENTS OF COMMERCE PUBLIC SCHOOLS 1901-1912. Compiled by F.T. Ingmire. $8.95. Ingmire.

HUNT COUNTY, TEXAS RECORD BOOK "D" Vol. I 1852-1855. St. Louis, 1981, 4to. $15.95. Ingmire.

JOHN W. McGUFFIN LOG BOOK OF PERSONAL PROPERTY AND POLL TAX, HUNT COUNTY, TEXAS 1873. Compiled by F.T. Ingmire. St. Louis, 1980, 98p.,index, 4to. $13.50. Ingmire.

MARRIAGE RECORDS OF HUNT COUNTY,TEXAS 1846-1880. Compiled by F.T. Ingmire. Creve Coeur,Mo. 1976. 57p.,index, 4to., $6.95. Ingmire.

MARRIAGE RECORDS OF HUNT COUNTY, TEXAS 1881-1889. Compiled by F.T. Ingmire. $8.95. Ingmire.

OCCUPATIONAL TAX REGISTER, HUNT COUNTY, TEXAS 1898-1908. Compiled by F.T. Ingmire. St. Louis, 1977. 113p.,4to. $9.95. Ingmire.

REGISTERED VOTERS OF HUNT COUNTY TEXAS 1867-1872. Compiled by F.T. Ingmire. St. Louis, 1980. 51p.,index, 4to. pc. $8.95. Ingmire.

HUTCHINSON

Created 1876 from Bexar County, organized 1901, named for early Texas jurist Anderson Hutchinson. County seat Stinnett; other towns include Borger, Phillips, Bunavista and Fritch. Bounded by Ochiltree, Moore, Sherman, Hansford, Roberts, Gray, Carson and Potter Counties.

BLACK GOLD AND RED LIGHTS [Borger]. By Jerry Sinise. Burnet, 1982. 152p.,ill.,biblio.,index, $8.95. Ranger.

HISTORY OF HUTCHINSON COUNTY. $47.25. Hutchinson.

IRION

Created and organized 1889 from Tom Green County, named for early Texas physician-politician Robert A. Irion. County seat Mertzon; other towns include Barnhart and Sherwood. Bounded by Reagan, Schleicher, Tom Green and Crockett Counties.

INVENTORY OF COUNTY RECORDS IRION COUNTY COURTHOUSE MERTZON, TEXAS. Compiled by Sharon Haney,et al. Austin, 1975, 104p. index 4to,pc. $1.00. TSL.

IRION COUNTY HISTORY. By Irion County Museum and Historical Society. San Angelo,Tx. 1978. 582p.,$25.00. Irion.

JACK

Created 1856 from Cooke County, organized 1857, named for brothers William H. and Patrick C. Jack, pioneer Texas settlers. County seat Jacksboro; other towns include Perrin. Bounded by Archer, Parker, Clay, Montague, Wise, Palo Pinto and Young Counties.

FORT RICHARDSON, TEXAS (1867-1878) and the Mackenzie Trail. By W.W. Dennis. Jacksboro,Tx. 1964. 40p.,ill.,pc.$5.00.Ranger.

FOUR SCORE YEARS IN JACK COUNTY. Compiled by Gilbert T. Webb. Jacksboro,Tx. 1940. 34p.,ill.,4to.pc.$15.00. Dennis.

HISTORY OF JACK COUNTY. By T.F. Horton. 1933. Facsimile reprint of 1975 with added preface. 155p.,ill. $15.00. Ranger.

JACKSBORO, TEXAS 1875-1975. Compiled by Bill Dennis. Jacksboro, 1975. $2.50. Jacksboro.

JACK COUNTY,TEXAS DROUTH SUFFERERS, 1887 AND TAX ROLLS 1858, 1859, 1861. Compiled by Mrs. L. Garner. $10.95.Ingmire.

JACK COUNTY,TEXAS MARRIAGE RECORDS BOOKS. Compiled by Mr. L. Garner. Books 1 & 2, $8.95; Book 3 1881-1889, $8.95; Book 4 1890-1900, $10.95. Ingmire.

JACK COUNTY, TEXAS MINUTES OF COMMISSIONERS COURT. Compiled by Mrs. Lucile Garner. $10.95. Ingmire.

JACK COUNTY, TEXAS MISCELLANEOUS RECORDS. Compiled by Mrs. L. Garner. $10.95. Ingmire.

JACK COUNTY, TEXAS PROBATE RECORDS. Compiled by Mrs. L. Garner. $8.95. Ingmire.

JACK COUNTY, TEXAS PROOFS OF HEIRSHIP. Compiled by Mrs. L. Garner. $10.95. Ingmire.

JACK COUNTY, TEXAS 1870 CENSUS. Compiled by F.T.Ingmire. St. Louis, 1980. 22 leaves. 4to. $8.95. Ingmire.

NINETY FOUR YEARS IN JACK COUNTY. By Mrs. Lasater Huckaby. Jacksboro,Tx. 1949. Reprint ed. 538p.,ill. $20.00. Ranger.

JACKSON

Created 1835, organized 1836, named for Andrew Jackson. County seat Edna; other towns include Ganado,Vanderbilt and Lolita. Bounded by Calhoun,Victoria,Lavaca,Colorado,Wharton and Matagorda Counties.

JACKSON COUNTY CENSUS RECORDS 1850. Index. $4.50.Heritage.

TEXAS CENSUS 1850 Vol. 2. Compiled by V.K. Carpenter. 1979. Reprint ed. pc. $10.00. Presley.

JACKSON COUNTY,TEXAS 1860 U.S. CENSUS. Compiled by F.T. Ingmire. 1981. 34p.,index.pc. $8.95. Ingmire.

JACKSON COUNTY, TEXAS 1870 U.S. Census. Compiled by F.T. Ingmire. 1980. 63p.,index, 4to. $10.95. Ingmire.

TWIN CENTENNIAL COMMEMORATIVE HISTORY. Edna-Ganado 1882-1982. By Commemorative Booklet Committee. Edna,Tx. 1982. 96p., ill.,4to,pc.$7.00. Twin.

JASPER

Created and organized in 1836, named for American Revolutionary soldier William Jasper. County seat Jasper; other towns include Buna, Kirbyville and Evadale. Bounded by Tyler, San Augustine, Sabine, Newton, Orange and Hardin Counties.

HISTORIC SITES IN JASPER COUNTY. By Jasper County Historical Commission. Jasper,Tx. 1979. Revised ed. $15.00. Stamps.

TEXAS CENSUS 1850. Vol. 4 . Compiled by V.K. Carpenter. 1979. Reprint ed. pc. $10.00. Presley.

JASPER COUNTY CENSUS RECORDS 1850. Index.$7.00.Heritage.

JASPER COUNTY CENSUS FROM 1850 to 1860. Compiled by Bertie Bryant. 1978. $7.35. Jasper.

JASPER COUNTY,TEXAS MARRIAGE RECORDS, 1849-1880. Compiled by F.T. Ingmire. $8.95. Ingmire.

JEFF DAVIS

Created and organized 1887 from Presidio County, named for Jefferson Davis. County seat Fort Davis; only other town Valentine. Bounded by Hudspeth, Presidio, Brewster, Pecos, Reeves and Culberson Counties.

FORT DAVIS ON THE TEXAS FRONTIER. Paintings by Captain Arthur T. Lee, Eighth U.S. Infantry. By W.S. Thomas. College Station, Tx. 1976. 109p.,ill.,biblio.,index. $10.00. Ranger.

JEFFERSON

Created 1836, organized 1837. Named for Thomas Jefferson. County seat Beaumont; other towns include Groves, Nederland, Port Arthur, Port Neches and Sabine Pass. Bounded by Chambers, Liberty, Hardin and Orange Counties, by Louisiana on the east and the Gulf of Mexico on the south.

BEAUMONT. A Chronicle of Promise. An Illustrated History. By J.W. Linsley and E.W. Rienstra. Beaumont, 1981. 190p.,ill.,biblio,index, 4to. $22.95. Johnson.

INVENTORY OF COUNTY RECORDS JEFFERSON COUNTY COURTHOUSE BEAUMONT, TEXAS. Compiled by Jefferson County Historical Commission. Denton, 1979. Three volumes, map,index, 4to. $9 for the three volumes. TSL.

JEFFERSON COUNTY, TEXAS CEMETERIES. Compiled by Mrs. Mildred S. Wright. Beaumont, Tx. Part I, 130p., 4to. $12.50; Part 2, 170p., map, 4to. $20; Part 3, 104p., map 4to $17.95. Wright.

TEXAS CENSUS 1850. Vol. 3. Compiled by V.K. Carpenter. 1979. Reprint ed. pc. $10.00. Presley.

JEFFERSON COUNTY, TEXAS 1850 CENSUS AND CONSORTS. Compiled by Swenson, index, pc. $9.95. Ingmire.

JEFFERSON COUNTY CENSUS RECORDS 1850. Index. $9.50. Heritage.

JEFFERSON COUNTY, TEXAS 1870 U.S. CENSUS. Compiled by F.T. Ingmire. St. Louis, 1980. 53p., index, 4to. $10.95. Ingmire.

JEFFERSON COUNTY, TEXAS MARRIAGE RECORDS 1837-1899. $11.95. Ingmire.

JEFFERSON COUNTY, TEXAS MARRIAGES Vols. A & B. $15.50. Southeast.

NEDERLAND 1898-1973. Diamond Jubilee. Compiled by Mrs. J.M. Fleming, et al. Nederland, Tx. 1973. 94p., ill., pc. $3.00. Nederland.

PORT ARTHUR. American Guide Series. By Writers Program of the WPA. Houston (1940) 164p., ill., index. Write. Port Arthur.

SHOWER OF BLESSINGS. By Garland D. Cutler. Beaumont, Tx. 1982. 130p., ill. 4to, pc. $10.00. Cutler.

JIM HOGG

Created and organized 1913 from Brooks and Duval Counties, named for Governor James Stephens Hogg. County seat Hebbronville; other towns include Guerra and Randado. Bounded by Zapata, Webb, Duval, Brooks and Starr Counties.

No Publications Located.

JIM WELLS

Created 1911 from Nueces County, organized 1912, named for attorney-developer James B. Wells, Jr. County seat Alice; other towns include Ben Bolt, Premont and Orange Grove. Bounded by Live Oak, San Patricio, Nueces, Kleberg, Brooks and Duval Counties.

No Publications Located.

JOHNSON

Created and organized 1854 from Ellis, Navarro and Hill Counties, named for soldier-politician-surveyor Middleton Tate Johnson. County seat Cleburne; other towns include Burleson, Alvarado, Joshua, Keene and Mansfield. Bounded by Parker, Ellis, Tarrant, Hill, Bosque, Hood and Somervell Counties.

JOSHUA. As It Was and Is. 1853-1976. By The Joshua Historical Committee. Cleburne, Tx. 1977. 198p., ill., 4to. $22.00. Joshua.

JOSHUA. As It Was and Is. Vol. 2. Centennial Edition. 1881-1981. Cleburne, Tx. 1981. 200p., ill., index to both volumes. 4to. $22.00. Joshua.

OLD NORTHWEST TEXAS. Navarro County 1846-1860. By N.T. Samuels and B.R.Knox. Ft. Worth. Two volumes, 863p.,ill.,biblio., index. $50.00. Fort Worth.

JONES

Created 1858, re-created 1876 from Bexar and Bosque Counties, named for Anson Jones. County seat Anson; other towns include Hamlin, Hawley and Stamford. Bounded by Stonewall, Haskell, Shackelford, Nolan, Taylor and Fisher Counties.

CHAMBER OF COMMERCE CENTENNIAL TABLOID. $8.00. Jones.

FIRST 100 YEARS OF JONES COUNTY, TEXAS. By Hooper Shelton and Homer Hutto Stamford, 1978. 304p.,ill. $14.50. Ranger.

THE OLD HOME PLACE. Farming on the West Texas Frontier. By David L. Caffey. Burnet,Tx. 1981. 224p.,ill.,index.$12.00. Ranger.

KARNES

Created and organized 1854 from Bexar, Goliad and San Patricio Counties. Named for Texas Revolutionary Henry Wax Karnes. County seat Karnes City; other towns include Kenedy, Panna Maria, Pawelekville, Falls City and Runge. Bounded by Atascosa, Wilson, Gonzales, DeWitt, Goliad, Bee and Live Oak Counties.

THE EARLY HISTORY OF PANNA MARIA, TEXAS. Lubbock, 1975. 69p.,ill.,biblio.,index,pc. $4.00. Tech.

KARNES COUNTY STORY. $1.00. Karnes.

THE LIFE AND TIMES OF THOMAS RUCKMAN. An Album of Southwest Texas Heritage. $1.85. Karnes.

KAUFMAN

Created and organized 1848 from Henderson County, named for David S. Kaufman, attorney-politician. County seat Kaufman; other towns include Crandall, Forney, Kemp, Mabank and Terrell. Bounded by Ellis, Dallas, Rockwall, Hunt, Van Zandt and Henderson Counties.

KAUFMAN. A Pictorial History. By Edward Cave. $24.95. Kaufman.

THE KAUFMAN CEMETERY, KAUFMAN, TEXAS. $14.95. Clay.

TEXAS CENSUS 1850. Vol. 14. Compiled by V.K. Carpenter. 1979. Reprint ed. pc.,$10.00. Presley.

KAUFMAN COUNTY CENSUS RECORDS 1850. Index.$6.00.Heritage.

KAUFMAN COUNTY HISTORY V. $30.00. Kaufman.

KAUFMAN COUNTY, TEXAS MARRIAGES 1848-1870. Book I & IA. Compiled by Exa Thomas. 40p.,4to.,pc.$5.00. Mesquite.

KAUFMAN COUNTY, TEXAS MARRIAGE INDEXES. Vol.I 1848-1880. Vol. 2 1881-1890. Vol. 3 1891-1900. $14.95 ea. volume. Clay.

Periodical: KAUFMAN COUNTY GENEALOGICAL QUARTERLY. Publication of the Kaufman County Genealogical Society. Write. Kaufman.

KENDALL

Created and organized 1862 from Blanco and Kerr Counties, named for journalist-author George Wilkins Kendall. County seat Boerne; other towns include Comfort. Bounded by Kerr, Gillespie, Blanco, Comal, Bexar and Bandera Counties.

HISTORIC IMAGES OF BOERNE, TEXAS. By Garland A. Perry. Boerne, Tx. 1982. 310p.,index, 4to. $24.00. Perry.

Periodical: NEWSLETTER. Quarterly of the Genealogical Society of Kendall County, Texas. $10/Year with membership. Boerne.

KENEDY

Created and organized 1921 from Cameron, Willacy and Hidalgo Counties. Named for Mifflin Kenedy. County seat Sarita, other town Armstrong. Bounded by Kleberg, Brooks, Hidalgo and Willacy Counties, and by Gulf of Mexico on the east.

INVENTORY OF COUNTY RECORDS KENEDY COUNTY COURTHOUSE SARITA, TEXAS. Compiled by Margaret Shuman,et al. Denton, Texas 1978. 125p.,map,index, 4to,pc. $1.00. TSL.

THE KING RANCH. By Tom Lea. Boston, 1957. Two volumes boxed, 838p.,ill.,notes, index. $150.00. Ranger.

PADRE ISLAND NATIONAL SEASHORE. A Guide to the Geology, Natural Environments and History of a Texas Barrier Island. By B.R. Weise and W.A. White. Austin, 1980. 94p.,ill.,biblio.,index, 4to,pc. $4.00. BEG.

KENT

Created 1876 from Bexar County, organized 1892, named for Andrew Kent, one of the "Thirty-two from Gonzales." County seat Jayton; other towns include Girard. Bounded by Garza, Crosby, Dickens,King, Stonewall, Fisher and Scurry Counties.

THE ESPUELA LAND AND CATTLE COMPANY. By W.C. Holden. 1970. 268p.,ill.,biblio.,index. $9.00. Ranger.

HISTORY OF KENT COUNTY, TEXAS. By Erma Black. Rotan, Tx. Projected for publication. Write. Black.

KERR

Created and organized 1856 from Bexar County, named for colonist James Kerr. County seat Kerrville; other towns include Hunt, Ingram, and Mountain Home. Bounded by Real, Edwards, Kimble, Gillespie, Kendall and Bandera Counties.

IN THE HEART OF THE HILLS. By W.B. Alderman. Austin,1966. Offset reprint from Texas Parade magazine. 8p.,4to,pc. $5.00. Ranger.

KERR COUNTY, TEXAS 1856-1976. By Clara Watkins. Kerrville, 1976. Revised ed. of Bennett's book. 343p.,ill.,index. $7.50. Kerr.

KIMBLE

Created 1858 from Bexar County, organized 1876, named for George C. Kimble, one of the "Thirty-two from Gonzales." County seat Junction; other towns include London, Cleo, Roosevelt and Segovia. Bounded by Sutton, Schleicher, Menard, Mason, Gillespie, Kerr and Edwards Counties.

RECORDED LANDMARKS OF KIMBLE COUNTY. Compiled by Kimble County Historical Survey Committee. Junction, $10.00. Junction.

KING

Created 1876 from Bexar County, organized 1874, named for William P. King, one of the "Thirty-two from Gonzales." County seat Guthrie; other towns include Dumont, Finney and Grow. Bounded by Stonewall, Dickens, Motley, Cottle, Foard, Knox, Haskell and Kent Counties.

INVENTORY OF COUNTY RECORDS KING COUNTY COURTHOUSE GUTHRIE,TEXAS. Compiled by Maurice G. Fortin,et al. Denton, Tx. 1980. 93p.,map,index,4to,pc. $3.00. TSL.

KING COUNTY. Windmills and Barbed Wire. Compiled by King County Historical Society. Quanah,Tx. 1976. 465p.,ill.,4to. $25.00 Ranger.

KINNEY

Created 1850 from Bexar County, organized 1874, named for Corpus Christi founder Henry L. Kinney. County seat Brackettville; other towns include Spofford. Bounded by Val Verde, Edwards, Uvalde, Zavala and Maverick Counties, and by Mexico on the southwest.

KINNEY COUNTY. 125 Years of Growth 1852-1977. Brackettville, Tx. 1977. 266p.,ill. 4to. $21.00. Kinney.

KLEBERG

Created and organized 1913 from Nueces County, named for soldier-politician Robert Justus Kleberg. County seat Kingsville; other towns include Ricardo and Riviera. Bounded by Nueces, Jim Wells, Brooks and Kenedy Counties, and by the Gulf of Mexico on the east.

THE KING RANCH. By Tom Lea. Boston, 1957. Two volumes boxed, 838p.,ill.,notes,index, $150.00. Ranger.

KLEBERG COUNTY,TEXAS. By Kleberg County Historical Commission. 1979. 1,023p. $30.00. Kleberg.

PADRE ISLAND NATIONAL SEASHORE. A Guide to the Geology, Natural Environments and History of a Texas Barrier Island. By B.R. Weise and W.A. White. Austin, 1980. 94p.,ill.,biblio.,index, 4to.,pc. $4.00. BEG.

KNOX

Created 1858 from Bexar and Young Counties, re-created 1876, organized 1886, named for Washington's first Secretary of War Henry Knox. County seat Benjamin; other towns include Goree, Knox City, Munday and Truscott. Bounded by Foard, King, Baylor, Throckmorton, Haskell and Stonewall Counties.

BETWEEN THE WICHITAS [History of Northern Knox County]. By Truscott Historical Preservation Society. Est. $30, to be released early 1983. Write. Truscott.

HISTORY OF ST. JOSEPH'S PARISH. Burnet. 200p.,4to.$11.00. Ranger.

KNOX COUNTY HISTORY. By Knox County History Committee. 1966. Revised ed. with added index. 422p.,ill. $20.00. Ranger.

MY HOME TOWN. A History of Munday, Texas. By Munday Historical Society. 1981. $15.75. Munday.

LAMAR

Created from Red River County 1840, organized 1841, named for Mirabeau B. Lamar. County seat Paris; other towns include Deport, Arthur City, Reno and Blossom. Bounded by Fannin, Delta,Franklin and Red River Counties, and by Oklahoma on the north.

FIRST SETTLERS OF LAMAR COUNTY, TEXAS. Compiled by Gifford White. pc. $12.50. Ericson.

INVENTORY OF COUNTY RECORDS LAMAR COUNTY COURT-HOUSE PARIS,TEXAS. Compiled by James Riney,et al. Denton,Tx. 1979. 249p.,map,index,4to,pc. $3.00. TSL.

LAMAR COUNTY CENSUS RECORDS 1850. Index.$16.50.Heritage.

TEXAS CENSUS 1850. Vol. 17. Compiled by V.K. Carpenter. 1979. Reprint ed. pc.,$10.00. Presley.

LAMAR COUNTY, TEXAS MARRIAGE RECORDS 1847-1874. Compiled by F.T. Ingmire. pc. $12.50. Ingmire.

PARIS FIRE OF 1916. By H.L. Hollis. Paris,Tx. 1982. 44p.,ill., index,4to.pc.$10.00. Paris.

THE PARIS TORNADO, APRIL 2, 1982. $5.95. Metro.

TORNADO: THE PARIS STORY IN WORDS AND PICTURES. $3.95. News.

TORNADO RAVAGES PARIS, TEXAS. $3.50. Pyramid.

LAMB

Created 1876 from Bexar District, organized 1908, named for Lt. G.A. Lamb, killed at San Jacinto. County seat Littlefield; other towns include Sudan, Olton, Earth and Spring Lake. Bounded by Bailey, Parmer, Castro, Hale, Lubbock, Hockley and Cochran Counties.

GEORGE W. LITTLEFIELD,TEXAN. By J.Evetts Haley. Norman, Ok., 1943, later ptg. 287p.,ill.,biblio.,index,pc.$7.95. Ranger.

A HISTORY OF LAMB COUNTY,TEXAS. By Evelyn P. Scott. 281p.,ill. $22.75. Ingmire.

LITTLEFIELD LANDS. Colonization on the Texas Plains, 1912-1920. Austin, 1968. 161p.,ill.,biblio.,index.$ 12.00.Ranger.

LAMPASAS

Created from Bell and Travis Counties and organized 1856, named for a Spanish word meaning lilies. County seat Lampàsas; other towns include Lometa and Kempner. Bounded by San Saba, Mills, Hamilton, Coryell, Bell and Burnet Counties.

RELIGHTING LAMPLIGHTS OF LAMPASAS COUNTY. By Jonnie Ross Elzner. 1974. 331p.,ill. $10.45. Lampasas.

LA SALLE

Created 1858 from Bexar County, organized 1880, named for French explorer. County seat Cotulla; other towns include Encinal, Fowlerton and Los Angeles. Bounded by Dimmit, Zavala, Frio, Atascosa, Duval, McMullen and Webb Counties.

No Publications Located.

LAVACA

Created and organized 1846 from Colorado, Gonzales, Jackson and Victoria Counties, named for Spanish "la vaca," " the cow." County seat Hallettsville; other towns include Moravia, Moulton, Sweet Home, Shiner and Yoakum. Bounded by Gonzales, Fayette, Colorado,Jackson, Victoria and DeWitt Counties.

THE FREE STATE OF LAVACA. By Paul C. Boethel. Hallettsville,Tx. 1977. 184p.,index.$10.00. Ranger.

LAVACA COUNTY CENSUS RECORDS 1850. Index.$7.00.Heritage.

TEXAS CENSUS 1850 Vol.6. Compiled by V.K. Carpenter. 1979. Reprint ed. pc.$10.00. Presley.

MARYLAND CATHOLICS ON THE FRONTIER. The Missouri and Texas Settlements. 954p.,$52.50. O'Rourke.

MISTER CHARLIE. Memoir of a Texas Lawman 1902-1910. By Charlie Munson. Austin, 1975. 122p. $8.50. Ranger.

OLE FOLEY. The Story of W.G.L. Foley (1780-1874) By Paul C. Boethel. Hallettsville,Tx. 1981. 72p.,pc.$4.00. Ranger.

LEE

Created and organized 1874 from Bastrop, Burleson, Fayette and Washington Counties, named for General Robert E. Lee. County seat Giddings; other towns include Dime Box, Old Dime Box and Lexington. Bounded by Williamson, Milam, Burleson, Washington, Fayette, and Bastrop Counties.

HISTORY OF LEE COUNTY,TEXAS. By Mrs. James C. Killen. Quanah, 1974. 501p.,ill. biblio. index. 4to. $25.00. Ranger.

LEON

Created and organized 1846 from Robertson County, named for empresario Martin de Leon. County seat Centerville; other towns include

Jewett, Buffalo and Normangee. Bounded by Robertson, Limestone, Freestone, Anderson, Houston, Brazos and Madison Counties.

A HISTORY OF LEON COUNTY. By J.Y. Gates and H.B. Fox. Centerville, Tx., 1936. Reprint of 1977. 36p.,pc. $3.00. Leon.

LEON COUNTY CEMETERY RECORDS Vol. I. 1982. 153p.,index, 4to,pc. $8.75. Leon.

LEON COUNTY CENSUS RECORDS 1850. Index.$8.00. Heritage.

TEXAS CENSUS 1850. Vol. 11. Compiled by V.K. Carpenter. 1979. Reprint ed. pc. $10.00. Presley.

LEON COUNTY,TEXAS CENSUS 1860. Centerville,Tx.,60p.,index, 4to,pc. $4.50. Leon.

LEON COUNTY HISTORICAL COLLECTIONS. Vol.I. Centerville, Tx. 100p.,index,4to,pc. $8.50. Leon.

LEON COUNTY HISTORICAL COLLECTIONS. Vol.2. Centerville, Tx. 100p. index, 4to, pc. $6.00. Leon.

LEON COUNTY HISTORICAL COLLECTIONS. Vol.3. Centerville, In preparation. Write. Leon.

Periodical: LEON COUNTY GENEALOGICAL SOCIETY NEWSLETTER. $10.00/Year. Leon.

LIBERTY

Created and organized 1836, named for Spanish municipality Villa de la Santisima Trinidad de la Libertad. County seat Liberty; other towns include Cleveland, Hardin, Hull, Dasietta and Dayton. Bounded by Harris, Montgomery, San Jacinto, Polk, Hardin, Jefferson and Chambers Counties.

ATASCOSITO CENSUS OF 1850. Index. $2.25. Liberty.

LIBERTY COUNTY CENSUS RECORDS 1850. Index. $9.50.Heritage.

LIBERTY COUNTY CENSUS OF 1850. Index. $10.00. Liberty.

TEXAS CENSUS 1850. Vol. 3. Compiled by V.K. Carpenter.1979. Reprint ed. pc. $10.00. Presley.

LIBERTY COUNTY CENSUS OF 1860. Index. $12.00. Liberty.

LIBERTY COUNTY CENSUS OF 1870. Index. $13.50. Liberty.

LIBERTY COUNTY CENSUS OF 1880. Index. $20.00. Liberty.

LIBERTY COUNTY, TEXAS CEMETERIES. Compiled by Mrs. M. S. Wright. Beaumont,Tx. Part I, 168p,maps,index,$15.50. Part 2, 181p.,maps,index, $17.95. Wright.

INVENTORY OF COUNTY RECORDS LIBERTY COUNTY COURTHOUSE LIBERTY, TEXAS. Austin, 1975. 134p.,index,4to,pc.$1.00.TSL.

LIBERTY, LIBERTY COUNTY AND THE ATASCOSITO DISTRICT. By Miriam Partlow. Austin, 1974. 369p.,ill.,biblio.,index,4to. $17.50 Ranger.

Periodical: THE CLEVELAND AREA PIONEER. Quarterly. $6.00 per year. CAGE.

LIMESTONE

Created and organized 1846 from Robertson County, named for native stone. County seat Groesbeck; other towns include Mexia, Ben Hur, Coolidge, Kosse, Thornton and Tehuacana. Bounded by Falls, Hill, McLennan, Navarro, Freestone, Leon and Robertson Counties.

A HISTORY OF PRAIRIE HILL. $8.00. Prairie.
LIMESTONE COUNTY CENSUS RECORDS 1850. Index. $12.00 Heritage.
TEXAS CENSUS 1850. Vol. 9. Compiled by V.K. Carpenter. 1979. Reprint ed. pc. $10.00. Presley.
TRINITY UNIVERSITY. A Record of One Hundred Years. By Donald E. Everett. San Antonio, 1968. 276p.,$5.00. Ranger.

LIPSCOMB

Created from Bexar County 1876, organized 1887, named for attorney-politician Abner S. Lipscomb. County seat Lipscomb; other towns include Booker, Darrouzett, Follett and Higgins. Bounded by Roberts, Hemphill and Ochiltree Counties and by Oklahoma on the north & east.

PIONEERS OF THE PRAIRIES. By Mildred Bieker. 1967. 211p., $15.00. Lipscomb.
DIMENSIONS OF PROGRESS. By Mrs. Lowell Bowdle. 1969. 320p., $15.00. Lipscomb.
HISTORY OF LIPSCOMB COUNTY, TEXAS. By Lipscomb County Historical Survey Comm. 1976. 676p. $22.50. Lipscomb.

LIVE OAK

Created and organized 1856 from San Patricio and Nueces Counties, named for native tree. County seat George West; other towns include Three Rivers, Whitsett and Oakville. Bounded by McMullen, Karnes, Atascosa, Bee, San Patricio, Jim Wells and Duval Counties.

GUSSETTVILLE CEMETERY. Live Oak County.$2.00.McWilliams.
LIVE OAK COUNTY BOOK I OF WILLS.$4.00. McWilliams.
THE PEOPLE'S HISTORY OF LIVE OAK COUNTY. By Ervin L. Sparkman. Mesquite,Tx. 1981. $35.00. Ide House.

LLANO

Created and organized 1856 from Bexar and Gillespie Counties, name is Spanish word for "plains." County seat Llano; other towns include Sunrise Beach, Kingsland and Tow. Bounded by Mason, San Saba, Burnet, Blanco and Gillespie Counties.

A CHURCH IN THE VALE. The Story of Valley Springs 1882-1982. By Mabel R. Osborn. 1982. 164p.,ill.,sources.4to.$17.50.Ranger.
COBWEBS AND CORNERSTONES. A History of Llano's Business District. By P.W. Almond and S.O. Franklin. Llano, 1976. 4to. $9.40. Llano.
INVENTORY OF COUNTY RECORDS LLANO COUNTY COURT-HOUSE LLANO,TEXAS. Denton, 1979. 183p,map,index,4to,pc.$1.00.TSL.
THE MEANEST KID IN TOWN. Memories of Llano 1890-1904.By Allan R. Townsend. Llano,Tx. $6.00. Llano.
Periodical: HILL COUNTRYGENEALOGICAL SOCIETY QUARTERLY. $10/Year. HCGS.

LOVING

Created 1887 from Tom Green County, organized 1931, named for "Dean of the Trail Drivers" Oliver Loving. County seat Mentone, only town. Bounded by Winkler, Ward and Reeves Counties, and by New Mexico on the north.

No Publications Located.

LUBBOCK

Created from Bexar District 1876, organized 1891, named for Colonel Thomas A. Lubbock of Terry's Texas Rangers. County seat Lubbock; other towns include Idalou, Abernathy, Shallowater, Slaton and Wolfforth. Bounded by Hockley, Lamb, Hale, Floyd, Crosby, Garza, Lynn and Terry Counties.

EVOLUTION OF A UNIVERSITY. Texas Tech's First Fifty Years. By J.G. Rushing and K.A. Nall. Austin, 250p., ill. cloth $9.95. Limited ed. in leather $20.00. Ranger.

FIFTY YEARS OF SERVICE TO WEST TEXAS AGRICULTURE. A History of Texas Tech University's College of Agricultural Sciences. By Donald E. Green. Lubbock, Tx. 1977. 182p., ill., biblio., index, $11.95. Tech.

A HISTORY OF LUBBOCK. Edited by Lawrence L. Graves. Lubbock, Tx. 1962. 692p., ill., biblio., index. $10.00. Ranger.

A HISTORY OF MEXICAN AMERICANS IN LUBBOCK COUNTY, TEXAS. By A.A. Tijerina. Lubbock, Tx. 1979. 73p., pc. $5.00. Tech.

LYNN

Created 1876 from Bexar County, organized 1903, named for W. Lynn, who died at the Alamo. County seat Tahoka; other towns include Wilson, New Home and O'Donnell. Bounded by Terry, Hockley, Lubbock, Crosby, Garza, Borden and Dawson Counties.

THE BEST DAMN TEACHER. By L.L. Loyd. Cisco, Tx. 1978. includes teaching experiences in Wilson, Tx. $9.95. Lloyd.

HISTORY OF LYNN COUNTY. By Frank P. Hill. In preparation for publication in 1983 or early 1984. Write. Lynn.

McCULLOCH

Created from Bexar County 1856, organized 1876, named for Ben McCulloch. County seat Brady; other towns include Mercury and Rochelle. Bounded by Concho, Coleman, Brown, San Saba, Mason, and Menard Counties.

HANDBOOK OF McCULLOCH COUNTY HISTORY. Vol. 1. Compiled by Wayne Spiller. Seagraves, Tx. 1976. 618p., ill., index, 4to. $17.00. Ranger.

IN THE SOUND OF THE BELL [Reminiscences of Rochelle, Tx] by C.C. Willoughby. N.Y. 1977. 262p., $7.95. Brady.

McLENNAN

Created and organized 1850 from Milam County, named for first settler Neil McLennan. County seat Waco; other towns include Bellmead, Mart, McGregor, Moody, West and Woodway. Bounded by Bosque, Limestone, Hill, Falls, Bell and Coryell Counties.

THE BEST DAMN TEACHER. By L.L. Lloyd. Cisco, 1978. includes teaching experiences in Waco. $9.95. Lloyd.

EARLY HOMES OF WACO. By L.J. Barnes. Waco, 1970. 2d Ptg. of 1981. $12.50. Historic.

EARLY WACO OBITUARIES (1874-1908) 520p.,$20.00. Waco.

THE HANDBOOK OF WACO AND McLENNAN COUNTY,TEXAS. Edited by Dayton Delley. Waco, 1972. 313p.,$10.00. Ranger.

LONE OAK CEMETERY & BATTLE CEMETERY. Compiled by M. Dulaney & M.B. McGaughy. 100p., $12.00. Shockley.

McLENNAN COUNTY CEMETERY RECORDS. Waco, 1981-1982. Vol.2,197p.,index $10.00; Vol. 3, 600p.,index $12.50; Vol. 4, 211p., index $15.00; Vol. 5, 200p.,index $15.00. Waco.

McLENNAN COUNTY, TEXAS MARRIAGE RECORDS. Waco,Tx. Vol. 2 Jan 1871-Jul 1892, 200p.,index. $15.00. Waco.

NINETEENTH CENTURY CHURCH BUILDINGS. By L.J. Barnes. $19.95. Historic.

A PICTORIAL HISTORY OF WACO. By Roger N. Conger. Waco, 1964. 292p.,ill.,4to. $12.50. Ranger.

WACO. Texas Crossroads. By P.W. Wallace. Due for publication. Write. Historic.

Periodical: THE FAMILY TREE. Publication of the Central Texas Genealogical Society. Write. Waco.

Periodical. HEART OF TEXAS RECORDS. Publication of the Central Texas Genealogical Society. Write. Waco.

McMULLEN

Created 1858 from Atascosa, Bexar and Live Oak Counties, organized 1862, reorganized 1877, named for empresario John McMullen. County seat Tilden; other towns include Calliham and Cross. Bounded by Frio, Atascosa, Live Oak, Duval, Webb and LaSalle Counties.

McMULLEN COUNTY HISTORY. 750p.,$50.00. McMullen.

MADISON

Created 1853 from Grimes, Leon and Walker Counties, organized 1854, named for James Madison. County seat Madisonville; other towns include North Zulch and Midway. Bounded by Leon, Houston,Walker, Robertson, Brazos and Grimes Counties.

MADISON COUNTY CEMETERIES. Compiled by The Generation Gap. In preparation. Write. Madison.

MADISON COUNTY METEOR REPRINT OF THE CIVIL WAR VETERANS. $15.00. Madison.

MARION

Created and organized 1860 from Cass County, named for American Revolutionary General Francis Marion. County seat Jefferson; other towns include Smithland and Berea. Bounded by Cass, Morris, Upshur and Harrison Counties, and by Arkansas on the east.

CADDO. A Survey of Caddo Indians in N.E. Texas and Marion County. By Mildred Gleason. 1981. $12.95. Jefferson.

CARPETBAGGERS, SCALAWAGS & OTHERS. By Traylor Russell. 1973. $10.95. Jefferson.

THE DEADLY JEWELS OF DIAMOND BESSIE. $1.50. Excelsior.

DIAMOND BESSIE AND THE ROTHCHILD TRIALS. Mt. Pleasant, Tx. 1971. 183p.,ill. $9.95. Jefferson.

HISTORY OF JEFFERSON, Compiled by McKay & Spellings. 1936. Price unknown. Write. Excelsior.

MARRIAGE AND DEATH NOTICES MARION COUNTY, TEXAS AND ENVIRONS 1853-1927. Compiled by Juanita D. Cawthon. 1980. 160p., index, 4to,pc. $16.50. Cawthon.

MARTIN

Created 1876 from Bexar District and organized 1884, named for Texas Revolutionary Wylie Martin. County seat Stanton; other towns include Ackerly. Bounded by Andrews, Gaines, Dawson, Borden, Glasscock, Howard and Midland Counties.

No Publications Located.

MASON

Created and organized 1858 from Gillespie County, named for Fort Mason. County seat Mason; other towns include Pontotoc, Katemcy and Streeter. Bounded by Menard, McCulloch, San Saba, Llano, Gillespie and Kimble Counties.

MASON AND MASON COUNTY. A History. By Stella Polk Gipson. Burnet, 1980. Revised ed. 203p.,ill.,index. $12.95. Ranger.

MASON COUNTY HISTORICAL BOOK. By Mason County Historical Commission. San Angelo, 1976. 384p., $20.00. Mason.

MASON COUNTY, TEXAS CENSUS FOR 1900. Compiled by Joyce Capps. 184p.,index, 4to. pc. $10.50. Capps.

MATAGORDA

Created 1836, organized 1837, name derived from Spanish for dense canebrakes. County seat Bay City; other towns include Matagorda, Palacios, Blessing, Van Vleck, Wadsworth and Cedar Lane. Bounded by Calhoun, Jackson, Wharton, Fort Bend and Brazoria Counties.

DEMING'S BRIDGE CEMETERY 1850, HAWLEY CEMETERY 1898, TRES PALACIOS BAPTIST CHURCH 1852. Compiled by Ruth Pierce & A.B. Pierce. Midfield, 1977. 2d ed. 112p.,pc. $5.00. Hurta.

MATAGORDA COUNTY CENSUS RECORDS 1850. Index, $6.00. Heritage.

TEXAS CENSUS 1850. Vol. 2. Compiled by V.K. Carpenter. 1979. Reprint ed. pc. $10.00. Presley.

1860 CENSUS OF HISTORIC MATAGORDA COUNTY,TEXAS. Compiled by Shirley Brown. 80p.,index,4to.pc. $10.00. Matagorda.

1894 & 1895 SCHOOL CENSUS OF MATAGORDA COUNTY, TEXAS. Transcribed by Mattie Lee & Jackie Jecmenek. 1982. $8.50. Matagorda.

INVENTORY OF COUNTY RECORDS, MATAGORDA COUNTY COURTHOUSE BAY CITY, TEXAS. Compiled by M.G. Fortin,et al. Denton,Tx. 1980 225p.,map,index,4to,pc. $3.00. TSL.

110 YEARS OF METHODISM. History of First United Methodist Church, Bay City, Texas. Bay City, Tx. 1980. $12.95. Bay.

OUR YESTERDAYS. A Photo Album of Bay City's Past. By The Junior Service League. Bay City,Tx. 1976. $5.00. Humphries.

Periodical: OAK LEAVES. Publication of the Matagorda County Genealogical Society. $15.00 per year with membership. Matagorda.

MAVERICK

Created 1856 from Kinney County, organized 1871, named for Samuel Maverick. County seat Eagle Pass; other towns include Quemado, El Indio and Normandy. Bounded by Kinney, Uvalde, Zavala, Dimmit and Webb Counties, and by Mexico on the west.

HISTORICAL HIGHLIGHTS OF EAGLE PASS AND MAVERICK COUNTY. By Ben Pingenot. Eagle Pass, Tx. 1971. 25p.,ill.,notes. 4to.,pc. $5.00. Downing.

MEDINA

Created and organized 1848 from Bexar County, named for Medina River. County seat Hondo; other towns include Devine, La Coste, Natalia, D'Hanis, Castroville and Quihi. Bounded by Uvalde, Bandera, Atascosa, Bexar, Frio and Zavala Counties.

MEDINA COUNTY CENSUS RECORDS 1850. Index. $6.00. Heritage.

TEXAS CENSUS 1850. Vol. 7. Compiled by V.K. Carpenter. 1979. Reprint ed. pc. $10.00. Presley.

THE STORY OF CASTROVILLE. By Ruth C. Lawler. Castroville, Tx. 5th ptg. 68p.,ill.,pc. $4.00. Lawler.

MENARD

Created 1858 from Bexar County, organized 1871, named for Michel B. Menard. County seat Menard; other towns include Fort McKavett. Bounded by Concho, McCulloch, Mason, Kimble, Sutton, Schleicher and Tom Green Counties.

THE APACHE MISSION ON THE SAN SABA RIVER. Its Founding and Failure.[reprint from Southwestern Historical Quarterly] Austin, 1914. 36p.,map,footnotes.pc. $15.00. Ranger.

FORT McKAVETT,TEXAS. Post on the San Saba. By Margaret Bierschwale. Salado,Tx. 1966. 134p.,ill.,biblio.,index. Tall 8vo. $15.00. Ranger.

MIDLAND

Created and organized 1885 from Tom Green County, named because of its location halfway between Fort Worth and El Paso. County seat Midland; other towns include Spraberry. Bounded by Andrews, Ector, Martin, Glasscock, Reagan and Upton Counties.

LAND OF THE HIGH SKY . By John Howard Griffin. Midland,Tx. 1959. 212p.,notes,references, index. $25.00. Midc.

Periodical: THE THORNY TRAIL. Semi-annual publication of the Midland Genealogical Society. Write. Midland.

MILAM

Created 1836 from Municipality of Milam, organized 1837, named for Ben Milam. County seat Cameron; other towns include Rockdale, Milano, Thorndale and Gause. Bounded by Bell, Falls, Robertson, Burleson, Lee and Williamson Counties.

MILAM COUNTY CENSUS RECORDS 1850. Index. $14.50.Heritage.

TEXAS CENSUS 1850. Vol. 9. Compiled by V.K. Carpenter. 1979. Reprint ed. pc. $10.00. Presley.

MILLS

Created and organized 1887 from Brown, Comanche, Hamilton and Lampasas Counties, named for Texas jurist John T. Mills. County seat Goldthwaite; other towns include Priddy and Mullin. Bounded by Brown, Comanche, Hamilton, San Saba and Lampasas Counties.

MILLS COUNTY. The Way It Was. By Hartal Blackwell. $13.50. Mills.

A NO MAN'S LAND BECOMES A COUNTY. By Flora Bowles Gatlin. $10.00. Mills.

MITCHELL

Created 1876 from Bexar District, organized 1881, named for Texas Revolutionists Asa and Eli Mitchell. County seat Colorado City; other towns include Loraine and Westbrook. Bounded by Howard, Borden, Scurry, Fisher, Nolan, Coke and Sterling Counties.

THE CENTENNIAL BOOK. Mitchell County Centennial 1881-1981. Edited by Patrice McKinney. Colorado City, Tx., 1981. 256p.,ill., index, pc. $1.00. Mitchell.

MONTAGUE

Created 1857 from Cooke County, organized 1858, named for surveyor-Indian fighter Daniel Montague. County seat Montague; other towns include Bowie, Ringgold and Nocona. Bounded by Clay, Jack, Wise and Cooke Counties, and by Oklahoma on the north.

EARLY RECORDS OF MONTAGUE COUNTY, TEXAS 1858-1879. Compiled by Navena H. Troxel. Richardson,Tx. 1982. 95p.,index,4to. pc. $12.00. Troxel.

PANORAMA OF NOCONA'S TRADE AREA IN MONTAGUE COUNTY. Saint Jo, Tx., 1976. $10.00. Nocona.

MONTGOMERY

Created and organized 1837 from Washington County, named for American Revolutionary General Richard Montgomery. County seat Conroe; other towns include Porter, Magnolia, New Caney, Montgomery and Willis. Bounded by Grimes, Walker, Liberty, San Jacinto, Harris and Waller Counties.

AUSTIN COLONY PIONEERS. Including History of Bastrop, Fayette, Grimes, Montgomery and Washington Counties. By Worth S. Ray. Austin, 1970. Reprint of 1949 ed. 378p.,ill.,index. $17.50. Ranger.

MONTGOMERY COUNTY CEMETERIES. Compiled by Montgomery County Genealogical Society. Conroe,Tx. Five volumes. $7.88 each. Montgomery.

MONTGOMERY COUNTY CENSUS RECORDS 1850. Index. $9.00. Heritage.

TEXAS CENSUS 1850. Vol. 10. Compiled by V.K. Carpenter. 1979. Reprint ed. $10.00. Presley.

MONTGOMERY COUNTY HISTORY. Compiled by Montgomery County Genealogical Society. Conroe,Tx. 1981. 633p.,ill. $49.50. Montgomery.

MONTGOMERY COUNTY TEXAS MARRIAGES 1838-1894. Conroe, Tx. 80p.,pc. $7.88. Montgomery.

Periodical: THE HERALD. Quarterly of the Montgomery County Genealogical Society. $7.00 per year. Montgomery.

MOORE

Created 1876 from Bexar County, organized 1892, named for Texas Navy Commodore E.W. Moore. County seat Dumas; other towns include Cactus, Sunray and Exell. Bounded by Hartley, Dallam, Sherman, Hansford, Hutchinson, Carson, Potter and Oldham Counties.

No Publications Located.

MORRIS

Created and organized 1875 from Titus County, named for legislator-jurist William Wright Morris. County seat Daingerfield; other towns include Cason, Lone Star, Naples, Rocky Branch and Omaha. Bounded by Bowie, Red River, Titus, Camp, Marion and Cass Counties.

No Publications Located.

MOTLEY

Created 1876 from Bexar District, organized 1891, named for San Jacinto casualty Dr. J.W. Mottley. County seat Matador; other towns include Flomot and Roaring Springs. Bounded by Briscoe, Hall, Cottle, Dickens, King, Crosby and Floyd Counties.

THE MATADOR LAND AND CATTLE COMPANY. By W.M. Pearce. Norman,Ok. 1964. Reissue. 288p.,ill.,biblio.,index. $20.00. Ranger.

NACOGDOCHES

Created 1836, organized 1837. named for Nacogdoches Indians. County seat Nacogdoches; other towns include Chireno, Garrison and Melrose. Bounded by Cherokee, Rusk, Shelby, San Augustine and Angelina Counties.

BY EARLY CANDLELIGHT. The Story of Old Milam Lodge #2. By Archie P. McDonald. $6.00. Ericson.

CITIZENS AND FOREIGNERS OF THE NACOGDOCHES DISTRICT 1809-1836. Compiled by Carolyn Ericson. Index. $12.50. Ericson.

FIRES AND FIREMEN OF NACOGDOCHES, TEXAS. 1840-1974. 250p.,ill. $10.00. Ericson.

THE HISTORY OF NACOGDOCHES COUNTY. By Richard W. Haltom. Austin, 1968. Reprint of 1880 ed. 73p. $7.50. Ranger.

MINUTES OF THE DISTRICT COURT OF NACOGDOCHES COUNTY, TEXAS. Book A. 1836-1839. Compiled by E.B. Reeves.$12.50.Ericson.

MUSTER ROLL OF RESERVE MILITIA IN NACOGDOCHES COUNTY 1870. 32p. $3.00. Ericson.

NACOGDOCHES. Wilderness Outpost to Modern City. 1779-1979. Burnet, 1980. $10.00. Ranger.

NACOGDOCHES ARCHIVES. 1835 Entrance Certificates. By Betty Fagan Burr. 53p.,index.pc.$8.50. Ericson.

NACOGDOCHES COUNTY. Abstract of All Original Texas Land Titles. $7.95. Ericson.

NACOGDOCHES COUNTY CEMETERY RECORDS. Five volumes. $12.50 per volume. Ericson.

NACOGDOCHES COUNTY,TEXAS CEMETERIES 1970-Sept 1980. 308p. $18.50. Muckleroy.

NACOGDOCHES COUNTY, TEXAS CENSUS 1847. Compiled by Carolyn Ericson. $2.00. Ericson.

NACOGDOCHES COUNTY, TEXAS CENSUS RECORDS 1850. Index $21.50. Heritage.

TEXAS CENSUS. Vol. 12. Compiled by V.K. Carpenter. 1979. Reprint ed. pc. $10.00. Presley.

NACOGDOCHES COUNTY, TEXAS CENSUS 1854. Compiled by Carolyn Ericson. $3.00. Ericson.

NACOGDOCHES COUNTY CENTENNIAL 1716-1936. Reprint ed. 24p.,ill.,pc. $1.50. Ericson.

NACOGDOCHES COUNTY MARRIAGE RECORDS 1881-1888. Compiled by Carolyn Ericson. Index, $7.95. Ericson.

NACOGDOCHES HEADRIGHTS. A Record of the Disposition of Land in East Texas 1838-1848. Compiled by Carolyn Ericson. 142p., index,pc. $20.00. Ericson.

OLD NACOGDOCHES IN THE JAZZ AGE. By Martha Anne Turner. Austin, 1976. 183p.,ill.,index. Cloth $12.50. Ltd. ed. $20.00. Ranger.

THE PEOPLE OF NACOGDOCHES COUNTY IN 1850. Compiled by Carolyn Ericson. $8.00. Ericson.

THE PEOPLE OF NACOGDOCHES COUNTY IN 1860. Compiled by Carolyn Ericson. pc. $10.00, cloth $12.50. Ericson.

THE PEOPLE OF NACOGDOCHES COUNTY IN 1870. Compiled b Carolyn Ericson. pc. $10.00, cloth $12.50. Ericson.

THE PEOPLE OF NACOGDOCHES COUNTY IN THE CIVIL WAR. 320p:,ill.,biblio.,index, 4to. $24.95. Ericson.

TALES FROM THE OLD STONE FORT. By Linda E. Devereaux. $2.50. Ericson.

Periodical: YESTERDAYS. Biannual publication of Nacogdoches Genealogical Society. $7.50 per year. NGS.

NAVARRO

Created and organized 1846 from Robertson County, named for Texas-Mexican patriot Jose Antonio Navarro. County seat Corsicana; other towns include Powell, Blooming Grove and Kerens. Bounded by Hill, Ellis, Henderson, Anderson, Freestone and Limestone Counties.

NAVARRO COUNTY CENSUS RECORDS 1850. Index.$11.50.Herit

TEXAS CENSUS 1850. Vol. 15. Compiled by V.K. Carpenter. 1979. Reprint ed. pc. $10.00. Presley.

NAVARRO COUNTY CEMETERY RECORDS. Vol.I. $12.00. NCGS.

NAVARRO COUNTY HISTORY. Compiled by Wyvonne Putnam. Corsicana, Tx., 1975-1982. Vol.1, 244p, $10.50. Vol.2,505p. $35.00, Vol.3 424p.,$19.95. Navarro.

OLD NORTHWEST TEXAS. Navarro County 1846-1860. By N.T. Samuels and B.R. Knox. Ft. Worth. Two Volumes. 863p.,ill.,biblio., index. $50.00. Fort Worth.

Periodical: NAVARRO LEAVES AND BRANCHES. Publication of the Navarro County Genealogical Society. $10.00 per year. NCGS.

NEWTON

Created and organized 1846 from Jasper County, named for Corporal John Newton of American Revolutionary fame. County seat Newton; other towns include Deweyville, Wiergate and Bon Wier. Bounded by Sabine, Jasper and Orange Counties, and by Louisiana on the east.

GLIMPSES OF NEWTON COUNTY HISTORY. Compiled by Newton County Historical Commission. 1982. $15.00. Newton.

INVENTORY OF COUNTY RECORDS NEWTON COUNTY COURTHOUSE NEWTON, TEXAS. Compiled by Newton County Historical Comm. Denton,Tx. 1978. 201p.,index,4to,pc.$1.00. TSL.

NEWTON COUNTY CENSUS RECORDS 1850. Index. $7.50.Heritage.

TEXAS CENSUS 1850. Vol. 3. Compiled by V.K. Carpenter.1979. Reprint ed. pc. $10.00. Presley.

NEWTON COUNTY TEXAS CEMETERIES. Compiled by Mildred S. Wright. $15.00. Southeast.

NEWTON COUNTY, TEXAS MARRIAGES 1846-1899. Compiled by F.T. Ingmire. Index.pc.$9.95. Ingmire.

THOMAS S. McFARLAND JOURNAL 1837-1840. By Thomas S. McFarland. 1981. 155p. $17.50. Ranger.

NOLAN

Created 1876 from Bexar and Young Districts, organized 1881, named for Philip Nolan. County seat Sweetwater; other towns include Roscoe, Blackwell and Nolan. Bounded by Sterling, Coke, Runnels, Concho, Menard, Schleicher, Irion and Reagan Counties.

HISTORY OF NOLAN COUNTY, TEXAS. By E.L. Yeats and Hooper Shelton. Sweetwater. 1975. 256p.,ill. $14.50. Ranger.

NUECES

Created and organized 1846 from San Patricio County, names for Nueces River. County seat Corpus Christi; other towns include Robstown,Port Aransas, Agua Dulce, and Bishop. Bounded by San Patricio, Jim Wells and Kleberg Counties, and the Gulf of Mexico.

CORPUS CHRISTI. Economic Impact of the Port. By R.H.Ryan and C.W. Adams. Austin, 1973. 70p. $4.00. BBR.

FIRE & HARD TIMES. A History of the First Volunteer Fire Company in Corpus Christi. Corpus Christi,Tx. 1980. pc. $5.00. Corpus.

INVENTORY OF COUNTY RECORDS NUECES COUNTY COURTHOUSE CORPUS CHRISTI,TEXAS. Compiled by R.T.Marcum, et al. Denton,Tx. 1977. Two vols.,map, 4to.pc. $2.00 for both. TSL.

NUECES COUNTY CENSUS RECORDS 1850. Index.$4.50. Heritage.

TEXAS CENSUS 1850. Vol. 2 Compiled by V.K. Carpenter. 1979. Reprint ed. pc. $10.00. Presley.

NUECES COUNTY TEXAS 1750-1800. A Bicentennial Memoir. By D.E. Kilgore. Corpus Christi,Tx. 1975. 10p.,maps,footnotes,pc. $3.00. Corpus.

Periodical: REFLECTIONS. Publication of the Coastal Bend Genealogical Society. $8.00 per year. Coastal.

OCHILTREE

Created 1876 from Bexar District, organized 1889, named for early Texas leader William B. Ochiltree. County seat Perryton; other towns include Booker and Farnsworth. Bounded by Hansford, Hutchinson, Lipscomb, Hemphill, and Roberts Counties, and by Oklahoma on the north.

WHEATHEART OF THE PLAINS. An Early History of Ochiltree County. Perryton, 1969. 653p.,ill.,index. $20.00. Ochiltree.

OLDHAM

Created 1876 from Bexar County, organized 1880, named for Texas politician Williamson S. Oldham. County seat Vega; other towns include Adrian, Wildorado and Tascosa. Bounded by Hartley, Moore, Potter, Randall and Deaf Smith Counties, and by New Mexico on the west.

INVENTORY OF COUNTY RECORDS, OLDHAM COUNTY COURTHOUSE VEGA, TEXAS. Compiled by Claire Kuehn,et al. Denton, 1978. 151p.,map,index,4to,pc. $1.00. TSL.

MAVERICK TOWN. The Story of Old Tascosa. By John L. McCarty. Norman, Ok. 1968. Enlarged edition. 287p., ill., biblio., index. $15.00. Ranger.

OLDHAM COUNTY, TEXAS 1881-1981. Lubbock, 1981. $50.00. Oldham.

TASCOSA. Historic sites in the Texas Panhandle. By Pauline & R.L. Robertson. 1977. 72p., ill., pc. $4.95. Paramount.

ORANGE

Created and organized 1852 from Jefferson County, named for George Patillo's orange grove. County seat Orange; other towns include Bridge City, West Orange, Vidor, Mauriceville and Pinehurst. Bounded by Newton, Jasper, Hardin and Jefferson Counties, and by Louisiana on the east.

INVENTORY OF COUNTY RECORDS ORANGE COUNTY COURTHOUSE ORANGE, TEXAS. Compiled by Nina Harden, et al. Denton, Tx. 1979. 235p., map, index. 4to. pc. $3.00. TSL.

ORANGE COUNTY, TEXAS CEMETERIES "Evergreen." $7.50 Southeast.

ORANGE COUNTY, TEXAS CEMETERIES, Part 2. $15.00. Southeast.

Periodical: LAS SABINAS. Quarterly of the Orange County Historical Society. $2.50 per issue. Orange.

PALO PINTO

Created 1856 from Bosque and Navarro Counties, organized 1857, named for Palo Pinto (Spanish "pointed stick") Creek. County seat Palo Pinto; other towns include Mineral Wells, Graford and Strawn. Bounded by Young, Jack, Parker, Hood, Erath, Eastland and Stephens Counties.

OLD NORTHWEST TEXAS. Navarro County 1846-1860. By N.T. Samuels and B.R. Knox. Ft. Worth. Two volumes. 863p., ill., biblio., index. $50.00. Fort Worth.

POSSUM KINGDOM COUNTRY. Graford, Tx. 1979. $15.00. Palo Pinto.

PALO PINTO CAMPFIRES. By Pete Normand. Ft. Worth, Tx. 1980. 128p., ill., pc. $7.95. Normand.

TIME WAS. By A.F. Weaver. $24.15. AFW

PANOLA

Created and organized 1846 from Harrison and Shelby Counties, name from Indian "ponolo" (cotton). County seat Carthage; other towns include Tatum, Panola and Beckville. Bounded by Harrison, Rusk, and Shelby Counties, and by Louisiana on the east.

PANOLA COUNTY CENSUS RECORDS 1850. Index. $15.50. Heritage.

PANOLA COUNTY, TEXAS CENSUS 1860. $25.00. Phillips.

PANOLA COUNTY, TEXAS. Index to "Deed Book A." $10.00. Phillips.

PANOLA COUNTY, TEXAS MARRIAGE RECORDS. $12.50. Phillips.

PARKER

Created and organized 1855 from Bosque and Navarro Counties, named for early settler and legislator Isaac Parker. County seat Weatherford; other towns include Springtown, Millsap, Azle and Aledo. Bounded by Palo Pinto, Jack, Wise, Tarrant, Johnson and Hood Counties.

OLD NORTHWEST TEXAS. Navarro County 1846-1860. By N.T. Samuels and B.R. Knox. Ft. Worth. Two volumes. 863p.,ill.,biblio., index. $50.00. Fort Worth.

Periodical: TRAILS WEST. Quarterly publication of the Parker County Genealogical Society. $7.50 per year. Parker.

PARMER

Created 1876 from Bexar District, organized 1907, named for the "Ringtailed Panther" Martin Parmer. County seat Farwell; other towns include Bovina, Friona and Lazbuddie. Bounded by Deaf Smith, Castro, Lamb and Bailey Counties, and by New Mexico on the west.

A HISTORY OF PARMER COUNTY. By the Parmer County Historical Society. Quanah, 1974. 414p.,ill.,4to. $25.00. Ranger.

PRAIRIE PROGRESS. By the Parmer County Historical Commission. Friona,Tx. 1981, 599p.,ill. 4to. $50.00. Parmer.

PECOS

Created 1871 from Presidio County, organized 1875, named for Pecos River. County seat Fort Stockton; other towns include Sheffield, Coyanosa and Iraan. Bounded by Brewster, Jeff Davis, Reeves, Ward, Crane, Crockett and Terrell Counties.

TEXAS' LAST FRONTIER. Fort Stockton and the Trans-Pecos 1861-1895. By Clayton Williams. College Station,Tx. 1982. 457p.,ill., biblio.,index. $19.50. Ranger.

PECOS COUNTY, TEXAS MARRIAGE RECORDS. Vol.1,1875-1925, $7.95; Vol.2, 1925-1938,$7.95; Vol.3 1939-1947,$7.95. Ingmire.

SELECTED CEMETERIES OF PECOS COUNTY, TEXAS. Compiled by Reeves. pc. $6.95. Ingmire.

POLK

Created and organized 1846 from Liberty County, named for President James K. Polk. County seat Livingston; other towns include Corrigan, Leggett, Camden and Moscow. Bounded by San Jacinto, Trinity,Tyler, Angelina, Hardin and Liberty Counties.

THE PICTORIAL HISTORY OF POLK COUNTY. Livingston,Tx. 1978. Revised ed. 400p., $25.00. Polk.

POLK COUNTY CENSUS RECORDS 1850. Index. $9.50. Heritage.

TEXAS CENSUS 1850. Vol. 4. Compiled by V.K. Carpenter.1979. Reprint ed. pc. $10.00. Presley.

POLK COUNTY TEXAS CEMETERY INSCRIPTIONS. Compiled by G.Barber & O.Jackson. Lufkin,Tx.1976. 248p.,map,index,4to.$17.50. Barber.

POTTER

Created 1876 from Bexar County, organized 1887, named for an early Texas character Robert Potter. County seat Amarillo; other towns include Bushland and Cliffside. Bounded by Hartley, Moore, Randall, Carson, Hutchinson, Armstrong, Deaf Smith and Oldham Counties.

HISTORY OF POTTER COUNTY. 1887-1966. By Della Tyler Key. Quanah, 1972. 2d Ed. 357p.,ill.,biblio.,index. $15.00. Ranger.

Periodical: THE REFLECTOR. Quarterly of the Amarillo Genealogical Society. $5 per year. Amarillo.

PRESIDIO

Created 1850 from Bexar County, organized 1875, named for Presidio del Norte (Spanish "Fort of the North"). County seat Marfa; other towns include Presidio and Redford. Bounded by Brewster and Jeff Davis Counties, and by Mexico on the south.

BARONIAL FORTS OF THE BIG BEND. Ben Leaton, Milton Faver, and Their Private Forts in Presidio County. By Leavitt Corning,Jr. San Antonio, 1969. 2d Ptg. 146p.,ill.,biblio.,index. $4.00. Ranger.

SPUR RANCH and Other Circles of Time. Essays. By Evelyn Mellard. Salado,Tx. 1977. 206p.,ill. $15.00. Fletcher.

RAINS

Created and organized 1870 from Hopkins, Hunt and Wood Counties, named for Texas legislator Emory Rains. County seat Emory; other towns include Alba, Point and East Tawakoni. Bounded by Hunt, Van Zandt, Hopkins and Wood Counties.

HISTORY OF RAINS COUNTY. 1981. $35.00. Rains.

RAINS COUNTY, TEXAS CEMETERY INSCRIPTIONS. Vol. 1. index, pc. $9.95. Ingmire.

RAINS COUNTY, TEXAS MARRIAGE RECORDS 1879-1900. $8.95. Ingmire.

RANDALL

Created 1876 from Bexar District, organized 1889, named for Confederate General Horace Randal. County seat Canyon; other towns include Umbarger. Bounded by Potter, Carson, Armstrong, Swisher, Deaf Smith, Castro and Oldham Counties.

THE RANDALL COUNTY STORY. By Mrs. C.W. Warwick.Hereford, 1969. 360p.,ill.,index.4to. $12.50. Ranger.

REAGAN

Created and organized 1903 from Tom Green County, named for surveyor --Jurist John H. Reagan. County seat Big Lake; other towns include Best, Santa Rita, Texon and Stiles. Bounded by Midland, Glasscock, Tom Green, Sterling, Irion, Crockett and Upton Counties.

THE REAGAN COUNTY STORY. A History of Reagan County, Texas. By J.L. Werst,Jr. Seagraves,Tx. 1974. 276p.,ill.,index, 4to. $12.50. Ranger.

SANTA RITA. The University of Texas Oil Discovery. By M.W. Schwettmann. Austin, 1943. Reprint of 1958. 43p.,ill. $7.50. Ranger.

REAL

Created and organized 1913 from Bandera, Kerr and Edwards Counties. Named for rancher-politician Julius Real. County seat Leakey; other towns include Camp Wood. Bounded by Edwards, Kerr, Bandera and Uvalde Counties.

No Publications Located.

RED RIVER

Created 1836, organized 1837, named for Red River. County seat Clarksville; other towns include Kahawha, Bogata, Annona and Detroit. Bounded by Bowie, Morris, Titus, Franklin, Hopkins and Lamar Counties, and by Oklahoma on the north.

THE FIRST SETTLERS OF RED RIVER COUNTY,TEXAS. Compiled by Gifford White. St. Louis, 1981. 76p.,maps,index.4to $12.50. Ingmire.

RED RIVER COUNTY CENSUS RECORDS 1850. Index. $14.50. Heritage.

1860 FEDERAL CENSUS OF RED RIVER COUNTY,TEXAS. Compiled by M.S. Lane & E.B. Booth. 1978. 110p.,4to. pc. $10.00. Lane.

RED RIVER COUNTY,TEXAS MARRIAGE RECORDS 1845-1881. Compiled by the Mesquite Genealogical Society. Index. $12.50. Ericson.

REEVES

Created 1883 from Pecos County, organized 1884, named for rancher-soldier-legislator George R. Reeves. County seat Pecos; other towns include Balmorhea and Toyah. Bounded by Loving, Ward, Pecos, Jeff Davis and Culberson Counties, and by New Mexico on the north.

PECOS. A History of the Pioneer West. Seagraves,Tx. 1978 & 1981. Two volumes, 401 & 223pp. ill.,biblio.,index. 4to. $32.00 for both. Ranger.

REFUGIO

Created 1836, organized 1837, named for Nuestra Senora del Refugio Mission. County seat Refugio; other towns include Austwell, Tivoli and Woodsboro. Bounded by Aransas, San Patricio, Bee, Goliad, Victoria and Calhoun Counties.

REFUGIO COUNTY CENSUS RECORDS 1850.Index.$4.50.Heritage.

REFUGIO COUNTY,TEXAS 1870 CENSUS. $10.95. Ingmire.

REFUGIO COUNTY,TEXAS MARRIAGE RECORDS 1839-1881. $10.95. Ingmire.

ROBERTS

Created from Bexar District 1876, organized 1889, named for noted Texans John S. and Oran M. Roberts. County seat Miami; other towns include Wayside and Lora. Bounded by Gray, Carson, Hutchinson, Hemphill, Hansford, Ochiltree, Lipscomb and Wheeler Counties.

A HISTORY OF MIAMI AND ROBERTS COUNTY. Miami,Tx. 461p., ill. $25.00. Miami.

ROBERTSON

Created 1837 from Milam County, organized 1838, named for empresario Sterling C. Robertson. County seat Franklin; other towns include Bremond, Benchley, Hearne, Calvert and New Baden. Bounded by Brazos, Leon, Madison, Limestone, Falls, Milam and Burleson Counties.

CEMETERIES IN ROBERTSON COUNTY. Compiled by V. Corn. Houston, 1980. $23.00. Love.

HEARNE ON THE BRAZOS. By N.L. & N.L.,Jr. McCarver. San Antonio,Tx.1958. $10.00. McCarver.

A HISTORY OF THE FIRST BAPTIST CHURCH, CALVERT, TEXAS. 1869-1972. By Gladys J. Casimir. pc. $3.00. Calvert.

A HISTORY OF THE GRACE METHODIST CHURCH OF BREMOND, TEXAS AND REMINISCENCES 1868-1978. By James L. Turner. Waco, 1978. $10.00. Turner.

A HISTORY OF ROBERTSON COUNTY, TEXAS. By J.W. Baker. $12.50. Citizens.

THE NATIONAL HOTEL. By Ruth R. Lemming. 1982.$10.00.Lemming.

ROBERTSON COUNTY CENSUS RECORDS 1850. Index. $4.50 Heritage.

TEXAS CENSUS 1850 Vol. 9. Compiled by V.K. Carpenter. 1979. Reprint ed. pc. $10.00. Presley.

ROBERTSON COUNTY, TEXAS MARRIAGE RECORDS 1838-1875. Compiled by F.T. Ingmire. St.Louis, 1980. 58p.,4to.$10.95. Ingmire.

ROUGH ROAD TO ETERNITY. By Frank Boring. N.Y., 1979. $5.75. Boring.

RUSTLIN' ALONG THE BRAZOS. By Al Klement. N.Y., 1980. $7.95. Vantage.

ROCKWALL

Created and organized 1873 from Kaufman County, named for rock wall which outcrops at several points. County seat Rockwall; other towns include Fate, Heath, Chisholm and Royse City. Bounded by Kaufman, Dallas, Collin, and Hunt Counties.

CEMETERY INSCRIPTIONS OF ROCKWALL COUNTY,TEXAS. Compiled by Sandra H. Tedford. Farmersville,Tx.,1979. 265p.,index, 4to. pc. $14.75. Search.

1880 CENSUS OF ROCKWALL COUNTY, TEXAS. 1982. 100p.,index, 4to,pc. $12.50. Search.

ROCKWALL COUNTY TEXAS 1873-1976. Condensed History of Rockwall County. 1976. 32p.,pc. $3.00. Rockwall.

ROCKWALL COUNTY, TEXAS MARRIAGE RECORDS 1876-1894. Compiled by Mesquite Genealogical Society. $7.50. Ingmire.

RUNNELS

Created from Bexar and Travis Counties 1858, organized 1880, named for planter-legislator Hiram G. Runnels. County seat Ballinger; other towns include Rowena, Wingate and Winters. Bounded by Coke, Nolan, Taylor, Coleman, Concho and Tom Green Counties.

THE ROWENA COUNTRY. A Short History. By A.E. Skinner. Quanah, Tx. 1973. 235p.,ill.,biblio.,index. $12.00. Ranger.

RUNNELS IS MY COUNTY. By Charlsie Poe. San Antonio,Tx. 1970. $10.00. Runnels.

RUSK

Created and organized 1843 from Nacogdoches County, named for Texas politician Thomas J. Rusk. County seat Henderson; other towns include Joinerville, Overton, New London, Mount Enterprise, Tatum and Laird Hill. Bounded by Cherokee, Nacogdoches, Panola, Shelby, Harrison, Gregg and Smith Counties.

A BOUNDLESS PRIVELEGE. Growing Up in Henderson,Texas. By Oren Arnold. Austin, 174p.,ill. $10.00. Ranger.

MARRIAGE RECORDS OF RUSK COUNTY,TEXAS 1843-1877. Compiled by F.T. Ingmire. St. Louis, 1979. 98p.,index,4to,pc.$10.95. Ingmire.

NEW LONDON SCHOOL EXPLOSION, 1937. One Woman's Memory of Orange and Green. By Lorine Aylks Bright. Burnet,Tx. 240p.,ill. index. $11.00. Ranger.

RUSK COUNTY CENSUS RECORDS 1850. Index. $34.50.Heritage.

RUSK COUNTY, TEXAS 1850 CENSUS. Compiled by Mary F. Dunn. $10.95. Ingmire.

TEXAS CENSUS 1850. Vol. 13. Compiled by V.K. Carpenter.1979. Reprint ed. pc. $10.00. Presley.

Publication: RUSK COUNTY ECHOES. Monthly newsletter of the Rusk County Genealogical Society. $9.00 per year. RCGS.

SABINE

Created and organized 1837, named for the Spanish word for Cypress. County seat Hemphill; other towns include Milam, Geneva, Bronson and Pineland. Bounded by Shelby, San Augustine, Jasper and Newton Counties, and by Louisiana on the east.

HISTORY AND TAX RECORDS OF THE SABINE DISTRICT AND SABINE COUNTY,TEXAS. Compiled by Blanche Toole. 1981. $10.00. Sabine.

MINUTES 1858-1890 FIRST BAPTIST CHURCH, HEMPHILL,TEXAS. Compiled by Di Ann Vick. 232p.,pc. $12.50. Ingmire.

SABINE COUNTY CENSUS RECORDS 1850. Index. $9.50. Heritage.

TEXAS CENSUS 1850. Vol. 4. Compiled by V.K.Carpenter. 1979. Reprint ed. pc. $10.00. Presley.

1880 SABINE COUNTY CENSUS. Compiled by B.F. Toole. Hemphill, Tx. 1978. 115p.,4to. $10.00. Sabine.

SAN AUGUSTINE

Created 1836, organized 1837, named for Spanish municipality of San Augustine. County seat San Augustine; other towns include Broaddus and Macune. Bounded by Angelina, Nacogdoches, Shelby, Sabine, Tyler and Jasper Counties.

FIRST UNITED METHODIST CHURCH, San Augustine,Texas. 1837-1976. By B.P. Richey. $5.00. First United.

FROM DARKNESS TO LIGHT. The Story of the First Baptist Church of San Augustine, Texas. By Eva Jones. San Antonio, 1970. 106p.,ill. $6.95. EJ.

HISTORIC HOMES OF SAN AUGUSTINE. By Ann Clark. Austin, $15.00. Ranger.

SAN AUGUSTINE COUNTY CENSUS RECORDS 1850. Index. $12.50 Heritage.

TEXAS CENSUS 1850. Vol. 4. Compiled by V.K. Carpenter. 1979. Reprint ed. pc. $10.00. Presley.

SAN AUGUSTINE COUNTY, TEXAS MARRIAGE RECORDS. 1837-1880. Compiled by F.T. Ingmire. St. Louis, 1980. 57p., index,4to. $6.95. Ingmire.

SAN JACINTO

Created 1869 from Montgomery, Polk, Walker and Liberty Counties, organized 1870, named for the Battle of San Jacinto. County seat Coldspring; other towns include Shepherd and Oakhurst. Bounded by Polk, Walker, Trinity, Liberty, and Montgomery Counties.

A HISTORY OF SAN JACINTO COUNTY FAMILIES.$35.00.SanJac.

SAN PATRICIO

Created 1836, organized 1837, named for San Patricio Municipality. County seat Sinton; other towns include Edroy, Mathis, Gregory, Taft, Ingleside, Odem and Portland. Bounded by Aransas, Refugio, Nueces, Live Oak and Jim Wells Counties.

ARANSAS PASS,TEXAS. By Harriett Johnson,et al. Aransas Pass, Texas, 1976. 321p.,ill.pc. $5.00. Ranger.

THE FORGOTTEN COLONY. San Patricio de Hibernia. By Rachel H. Hebert. Burnet, 472p.,ill.,index. $25.00. Ranger.

SAN PATRICIO COUNTY CENSUS RECORDS 1850. Index. $4.50. Heritage.

THE TAFT RANCH. A Texas Principality. By A. Ray Stephens. Austin, 1964. 295p.,ill.,biblio.,index.$ 15.00. Ranger.

TEXAS CENSUS 1850. Vol. 2. Compiled by V.K. Carpenter.1979. Rerprint ed. pc. $10.00. Presley.

SAN SABA

Created and organized 1856 from Bexar County, named for San Saba River. County seat San Saba; other towns include Bend, Cherokee and Richland Springs. Bounded by McCulloch, Brown, Mills, Lampasas, Burnet, Llano and Mason Counties.

THE CALL OF SAN SABA. A History of San Saba County. By Alma W. Hamrick. Austin, 1969. 2d Ed. 381p.,index. $12.50. Ranger.

SCHLEICHER

Created 1887 from Crockett County, organized 1901, named for colonist and surveyor Gustav Schleicher. County seat Eldorado; no other towns. Bounded by Irion, Tom Green, Concho, Menard, Kimble,Sutton and Crockett Counties.

HISTORY OF SCHLEICHER COUNTY. San Angelo. 1979. 643p., ill. $30.00. Schleicher.

INVENTORY OF COUNTY RECORDS SCHLEICHER COUNTY COURTHOUSE ELDORADO, TEXAS. Compiled by J.W. Bates,et al. Denton,1979. 175p.,map, index, 4to. pc. $1.00. TSL.

SCHLEICHER COUNTY or Eighty Years of Development in Southwest Texas. By R.D. Holt. Eldorado,Tx. 1930. 110p.,ill.,pc. $40.00. Ranger.

SCURRY

Created in 1876 from Bexar District,organized 1884, named for Confederate General William R. Scurry. County seat Snyder; other towns include Fluvanna, Ira and Dermott. Bounded by Garza, Kent, Fisher, Nolan, Mitchell, Howard and Borden Counties.

FROM BUFFALO TO OIL. History of Scurry County,Texas. By Homer Shelton. 1973. 272p.,ill.,index. $12.50. Ranger.

SHACKELFORD

Created 1858 from Bosque County, organized 1874, named for John Shackelford, who was spared at Goliad because of his medical ability. County seat Albany; other towns include Fort Griffin and Moran. Bounded by Jones, Haskell, Throckmorton, Stephens, Eastland, Taylor and Callahan Counties.

INVENTORY OF COUNTY RECORDS SHACKELFORD COUNTY COURTHOUSE ALBANY, TEXAS. Compiled by D.M. Ferrier,et al.Denton, 1977. 157p.,map,index,4to,pc. $1.00. TSL.

SHACKELFORD COUNTY 1874-1974. By Shackelford County Historical Survey Committee. Albany, 1974. 28 unn. pages., ill.,4to,pc.$2.50. Albany.

SHACKELFORD COUNTY SKETCHES. By Don H. Biggers. Edited and annotated by Joan Farmer. Albany,Tx. 1974. Originally pub. in 1908. 114p.,frontis.,index. $12.50. Albany.

Publication: OLD TIMER. Publication of the Albany High School Junior Historians. $4.00. Albany HS.

SHELBY

Created 1836, organized 1837, named for American Revolutionary Isaac Shelby. County seat Center; other towns include Shelbyville, Joaquin, Patroon, Tenaha and Timpson. Bounded by Panola, Rusk, Nacogdoches, San Augustine and Sabine Counties, and by Louisiana on the east.

FIRST SETTLERS OF SHELBY AND HARRISON COUNTY,TEXAS Compiled by Gifford White. $12.50. Ericson.

LAND CERTIFICATES FOR SHELBY AND HARRISON COUNTIES, TEXAS 1838-1840. Compiled by Gifford White. Index,pc. $12.50. Ingmire.

SHELBY COUNTY CENSUS RECORDS 1850. Index. $19.00.Heritage.

TEXAS CENSUS 1850. Vol. 12. Compiled by V.K. Carpenter. 1979 Reprint ed. pc. $10.00. Presley.

SHELBY COUNTY SAMPLER. By Patricia R. McCoy. 1982. 179p., ill.,biblio.,index. $20.00. McCoy.

SHERMAN

Created 1876 from Bexar County, organized 1889, named for San Jacinto hero Sydney Sherman. County seat Stratford; other towns include Texhoma. Bounded by Dallam, Hartley, Moore, Hutchinson and Hansford Counties, and by Oklahoma on the north.

GOD, GRASS AND GRIT. History of the Sherman County Trade Area. Compiled by M. Albert. Two volumes. 4to. $12.50 each. Frizzell.

SMITH

Created and organized 1846 from Nacogdoches County, named for Texas Revolutionary General James Smith. County seat Tyler; other towns include Arp, Troup, Whitehorse, Bullard and Lindale. Bounded by Van Zandt, Wood, Upshur, Gregg, Rusk, Cherokee and Henderson Counties.

BOOMING, BLOOMING TYLER. By Keith Elliott. Austin, 1968. Offset reprint from Texas Parade Magazine. 8p.,ill.,pc. $5.00. Ranger.

CEMETERY RECORDS SMITH COUNTY, TEXAS. Oakwood and Rosehill. $10.00. East.

PINE BARK AND SPRING WATER. A History of Pine Springs, Texas. Ed. by V.E. Hardy. 1980. 250p.,ill.,index. $15.00.Shomburger.

SMITH COUNTY CENSUS RECORDS 1850. Index. $20.50.Heritage.

TEXAS CENSUS 1850. Vol. 14. Compiled by V.K. Carpenter. 1979. Reprint ed. pc. $10.00. Presley.

SMITH COUNTY, TEXAS CENSUS 1870. $10.00. East.

SMITH COUNTY, TEXAS IN THE CIVIL WAR. By Vicki Betts. Tyler,Texas. $10.00. Smith.

SMITH COUNTY, TEXAS MARRIAGES. 1846-1899. 2d Ptg. $10.00. East.

TYLER AND SMITH COUNTY. An Historical Survey. Compiled by the American Bicentennial Committee of Tyler-Smith County. Tyler,Tx. 1976. 287p., $17.50. Tyler.

Periodical: CHRONICLES OF SMITH COUNTY. Bi-annual publication of the Smith County Historical Society. $4 per issue. Smith.

SOMERVELL

Created and organized 1875 from Hood and Bosque Counties, named for Texas Revolutionary General Alexander Somervell. County seat Glen Rose; other towns include Nemo and Rainbow. Bounded by Erath, Hood, Johnson and Bosque Counties.

INVENTORY OF COUNTY RECORDS SOMERVELL COUNTY COURTHOUSE GLEN ROSE, TEXAS. Compiled by D.M. Ferrier,et al. Austin, 1974. 49p.,index, 4to pc. $1.00. TSL.

SOMERVELL. Story of a Texas County. By W.C Nunn. Ft. Worth, 1975. 258p.,ill.,biblio.,index. $10.00. Ranger.

STARR

Created and organized 1848 from Nueces County, named for James H. Starr of Texas Revolutionary fame. County seat Rio Grande City; other towns include Falcon Heights, Roma-Los Saenz and Grulla. Bounded by Zapata, Jim Hogg, Brooks and Hidalgo Counties, and by Mexico on the south.

TEXAS CENSUS 1850. Vol.1. Compiled by V.K. Carpenter. 1979. Reprint ed. pc. $10.00. Presley.

STEPHENS

Created from Bosque County 1858 as Buchanan County, but name was changed in 1861 to honor Alexander Stephens, organized 1876. County seat Breckenridge; other towns include Caddo and Gunsight. Bounded by Shackelford, Throckmorton, Young, Palo Pinto and Eastland Counties.

DOODLE BUG AND CACTUS BERRIES. A Historical Sketch of Stephens County. By Betty Elliott. Quanah, 1975. 147p.,ill.,index, $8.00. Ranger.

JOHN VAIL BALLADS. By John Vail. $7.95. Peeler.

LANTERN IN THE VALLEY. By Betty Hanna. 1981. $6.95. Swenson.

STERLING

Created and organized 1891 from Tom Green County, named for Indian fighter-rancher W.S. Sterling. County seat Sterling City; other town is Broome. Bounded by Glasscock, Howard, Mitchell, Coke, Tom Green and Reagan Counties.

INVENTORY OF COUNTY RECORDS STERLING COUNTY COURTHOUSE STERLING CITY, TEXAS. Denton,Tx. 1979. 155p.,map,index, 4to, pc. $1.00. TSL.

MILLING AROUND STERLING COUNTY. By Sterling County Historical Commission. 1976. Revised edition 1980. 382p. $20.00. Sterling.

STONEWALL

Created 1876 from Bexar County, organized 1888, named for Stonewall Jackson. County seat Aspermont; other towns include Old Glory, Peacock and Swenson. Bounded by Kent, Dickens, King, Knox, Haskell, Jones and Fisher Counties.

No Publications Located.

SUTTON

Created 1887 from Crockett County, organized 1890, named for Confederate Lieutenant Colonel John S. Sutton, who was killed at Val Verde. County seat Sonora, the only town. Bounded by Crockett, Schleicher, Menard, Kimble, Edwards and Val Verde Counties.

WILL CARVER, OUTLAW. By John Eaton. San Angelo. 1972.141p. ill.,index, pc. $10.00. Ranger.

SWISHER

Created 1876 from Bexar and Young Districts, organized 1890, named for Texas Revolutionary figure James G. Swisher. County seat Tulia; other towns include Happy, Kress and Claytonville. Bounded by Hale, Castro, Floyd, Briscoe, Armstrong and Randall Counties.

WINDMILLING. 101 Years of Swisher County,Texas History 1876-1977. By Swisher County Historical Commission. Tulia, 1976. 618p.,ill. 4to. $35.00. Swisher.

TARRANT

Created 1849 from Navarro County, organized 1850, named for General E.H. Tarrant of the Texas Revolution. County seat Fort Worth; other towns include Arlington, White Settlement, Grand Prairie, Grapevine, Euless, Keller and Kennedale. Bounded by Wise, Denton, Dallas, Ellis, Johnson and Parker Counties.

AND WORK WAS MADE LESS...History of Texas Electric Service Company. By Vance Gillmore. $17.50. Ranger.

CEMETERIES OF NORTHEAST TARRANT COUNTY,TEXAS. By E.D. Cushman. 1981. 320p.,$23.00. Cushman.

FORT WORTH IN THE CIVIL WAR. By James Farber. Belton,Tx. 1960. 58p.,ill. pc. $5.00. Ranger.

HOW FORT WORTH BECAME THE TEXASMOST CITY. Ft.Worth, 1973. 214p., ill.,biblio.,index. 4to. $17.50. Ranger.

IN OLD FORT WORTH. By Mack Williams. Ft. Worth,Tx. 1977. $12.50. News-Tribune.

MORE THAN A CENTURY. A Pictorial Record of TCU. By Jim Corder. 1973. $8.00. Ranger.

OLD NORTHWEST TEXAS. Navarro County 1846-1860. By N.T. Samuels and B.R.Knox. Ft.Worth. Two volumes. 863p.,ill.,biblio., index. $50.00. Fort Worth.

TCU. A Hundred Years of History. By Moore. $10.00. Ranger.

TARRANT COUNTY CENSUS RECORDS 1850. Index. $4.50. Heritage.

TEXAS CENSUS 1850. Vol. 15. Compiled by V.K. Carpenter. 1979. Reprint ed. pc. $10.00. Presley.

Periodical: FOOTPRINTS. Quarterly of the Fort Worth Genealogical Society. $8.00 per year. FWGS.

Periodical: A TALE OF MID-CITIES. Quarterly of the Mid-Cities Genealogical Society. $8.00 per year. Mid-Cities.

TAYLOR

Created 1858 from Bexar and Travis Counties, organized 1878, named for the three Taylor brothers who died at the Alamo. County seat Abilene; other towns include Buffalo Gap, Merkel, Trent and Potosi. Bounded by Nolan, Fisher, Jones, Shackelford, Callahan, Coleman and Runnels Counties.

ABILENE. An American Centennial. By Fane Downs and Roy Flukinger. Abilene,Tx. 1982. $24.50. Ranger.

ABILENE REMEMBERED. By Reporter Publishing Co. Abilene, Tx. 1981. $18.45. Abilene.

A BAKER'S DOZEN. The Caseys of Tuscola, Taylor County, Texas. By Clifford B.Casey. Seagraves,Tx. 262p.,ill. 4to. $9.75. Ranger.

FROM TENT TO COMPUTER. A History of the Abilene Reporter News. By Ed Wishcamper. Abilene, Tx. 1981. $4.00. Abilene.

FUTURE GREAT CITY OF WEST TEXAS. Abilene 1881-1891. Abilene,Tx. 1981. 45p.,ill.,pc. $2.50. Richardson.

HISTORY OF ABILENE. Facts and Sources. By Fane Downs,et al. 1981. 101p.,pc. $6.00. McMurray.

MEMORABILIA. An Album of Early West Texas. By James Conley. Abilene, 1971. $2.50. Abilene.

A PERSONAL COUNTRY. By A.C. Greene. College Station,Tx. 1979. Reprint ed. 354p.,ill. $12.95. Ranger.

PIONEER DAYS. Two Views. By Tommie Clack and Kathryn Duff. Abilene,Tx. 1979. $15.10. Abilene.

PIONEER WOMEN OF ABILENE. By Vernon G. Spence. Burnet, 1981., 114p.,ill.,biblio. $10.00. Ranger.

POTOSI. The First Hundred Years. By Juanita Zachry. Abilene, Tx. 1973. $5.95. Zachry.

THE SETTLING OF A FRONTIER. A History of Rural Taylor County. By J.D. Zachry. Burnet, 1980. 280p.,ill.,index. 4to. $25.00. Ranger.

THIS MAN DAVID. A Southern Planter. By Juanita Zachry. Abilene, Tx.,1971. $9.95. Zachry.

WITH GOD IN THE LIGHT. A Biography of Cal C. Wright. By Joseph Stamey. Abilene,Tx. 1978. paper,$4.95, cloth $8.95. McMurry.

TERRELL

Created and organized from Pecos County 1905, named for Confederate General Alexander W. Terrell. County seat Sanderson; other towns include Dryden. Bounded by Brewster, Pecos, Crockett and Val Verde Counties, and by Mexico on the south.

TERRELL COUNTY, TEXAS. Its Past - Its People. Edited by Alice Evans Downie. 750p.,ill.,biblio.,index. 4to. $25.00. Terrell.

TERRY

Created 1876 from Bexar District, organized 1904, named for Texas Confederate Colonel Benjamin F. Terry. County seat Brownfield; other towns include Wellman and Meadow. Bounded by Yoakum, Hockley, Lubbock, Lynn, Dawson and Gaines Counties.

TERRY COUNTY CEMETERY RECORDS. $12.50. Kendrick.

THROCKMORTON

Created 1858 from Fannin County, organized 1879, named for Texas Governor James W. Throckmorton. County seat Throckmorton; other towns include Elbert and Woodson. Bounded by Baylor, Archer,Young, Stephens, Haskell and Shackelford Counties.

INVENTORY OF COUNTY RECORDS THROCKMORTON COUNTY COURTHOUSE THROCKMORTON,TEXAS. Compiled by M.G. Fortin,et al. Denton,Tx. 1980. 127p.,map,index,4to.,pc. $3.00. TSL.

TITUS

Created and organized 1846 from Bowie and Red River Counties,named for pioneer developer Andrew J. Titus. County seat Mount Pleasant; other towns include Talco, Winfield and Monticello. Bounded by Morris, Franklin, Red River and Camp Counties.

TITUS COUNTY CENSUS RECORDS 1850. Index.$18.00. Heritage.

TEXAS CENSUS 1850. Vol. 18. Compiled by V.K. Carpenter. 1979. Reprint ed. pc. $10.00. Presley.

TOM GREEN

Created 1874 from Bexar County, organized 1875, named for Confederate General Thomas Green, killed at Blair's Landing. County seat San Angelo; other towns include Carlsbad, Water Valley and Christoval. Bounded by Sterling, Coke, Runnels, Concho, Menard, Schleicher, Irion and Reagan Counties.

THE CONCHO COUNTRY. By Gus Clemens. $25.00. Mulberry.

FORT CONCHO. Its Why & Wherefore. By J.N.Gregory. pc. $2.50. Fort Concho.

FORT CONCHO IN 1877. By Susan Miles. $6.95. Fort Concho.

FORT CONCHO MEDICAL HISTORY. By W.M. Notson. $5.00. Fort Concho.

LAS FIESTAS PATRIAS. Biographic Notes on the Hispanic Presence in San Angelo,Tx. By Arnoldo DeLeon. San Antonio,1978. 30p., ill.,biblio. pc. Write. Angelo.

Periodical: STALKIN' KIN. Quarterly of the San Angelo Genealogical and Historical Society,Inc. $7.50 per year. San Angelo.

TRAVIS

Created 1840 from Bastrop County, organized 1843, named for William Barrett Travis. County seat Austin; other towns include Pflugerville, Manor, Westlake Hills, Rollingwood and Jonestown. Bounded by Bastrop, Blanco, Burnet, Williamson, Caldwell and Hays Counties.

AESCULAPIUS ON THE COLORADO. Medical Practice in Austin & Travis County 1839-1900. By Dr. James M. Coleman. Austin, $10.00. Ranger.

ALPHONSE IN AUSTIN. Translated by Katherine Hart. Austin, $10.00. Ranger.

AUSTIN. A Historical Portrait. By Larry Willoughby. Norfolk, Va. 1981. 208p., ill., biblio., index. 4to. $16.95. Donning.

AUSTIN. The Past Still Present. By Sue B. McBee. Austin, 1975. 129p., ill. $8.95. CM.

AN AUSTIN ALBUM. By Audray Bateman. Austin, 1978. 129p., ill. $17.50. Ranger.

THE AUSTIN ALMANAC and Guide to Central Texas. By Will and Carol Howard, editors. Austin, 1982. 55p. + calendar pages. pc. $4.95. Winter. A 1983 is in the press.

AUSTIN AND TRAVIS COUNTY. A Pictorial History 1839-1939. By Katherine Hart. Austin, 1975. 160p., ill. $17.50. Ranger.

AUSTIN PRESBYTERIAN THEOLOGICAL SEMINARY. A Seventy-fifth Anniversary History. By Thomas W. Currie, Jr. San Antonio, 1978. 285p. $12.00. Ranger.

AN AUSTIN SKETCHBOOK. By Tony Crosby. Austin, Tx. $12.50. Ranger.

EARLY TRAVIS COUNTY, TEXAS RECORDS. Compiled by Jane Sumner. Easley, SC 1978. 196p., index. $22.50. Ranger.

INVENTORY OF COUNTY RECORDS TRAVIS COUNTY COURTHOUSE AUSTIN, TEXAS. Compiled by Kate Adams, et al. Denton, Tx. 1978. Two volumes, map, index, 4to. pc. $2.00 for both. TSL.

KINGDOM COME! KINGDOM GO!. On the Texas Frontier. By M.J. Atkinson. Burnet, 200p., ill., biblio., index. $12.00. Ranger.

LIFE ON WALLER CREEK. By Joseph Jones. Austin, 1982. 331p. ill., index. $17.95. Ranger.

TRAVIS COUNTY CENSUS RECORDS 1850. Index. $14.00. Heritage.

TEXAS CENSUS 1850. Vol. 8. Compiled by V.K. Carpenter. 1979. Reprint ed., pc. $10.00. Presley.

THE UNIVERSITY OF TEXAS. A Pictorial Account of its First Century. By Margaret C. Berry. Austin, 1980. 452p., ill., index. $25.00. Ranger.

WATERLOO SCRAPBOOK. Collections of articles on early Austin. 1970-71, $2.50; 1971-72, $3.00; 1972-73, $3.00; 1973-74, $3.50; 1974-75, $3.50; 1975-76, $3.75. Austin.

Periodical: AUSTIN GENEALOGICAL SOCIETY QUARTERLY. $9.00 per year. AGS.

TRINITY

Created and organized 1850 from Houston County, named for Trinity River. County seat Groveton; other towns include Trinity and Carlisle. Bounded by Houston, Angelina, Polk, San Jacinto and Walker Counties.

JOURNEY TO JUBILEE. Groveton, Texas USA. By Groveton Ex-Students Association. Groveton,Tx. 1980. 363p.,4to. $19.95.Groveton.

TRINITY COUNTY CEMETERIES. $15.00. Trinity

TRINITY COUNTY, TEXAS CONFEDERATE PENSION APPLICATIONS. Compiled by F.T. Ingmire. $10.95. Ingmire.

TYLER

Created and organized 1846 from Liberty County, named for President John Tyler. County seat Woodville; other towns include Chester,Spurger, Colmesneil and Doucette. Bounded by Polk, Angelina, Jasper and Hardin Counties.

TYLER COUNTY CENSUS RECORDS 1850. Index. $9.00. Heritage.

TEXAS CENSUS 1850 Vol. 4. Compiled by V.K. Carpenter. 1979. Reprint ed. pc. $10.00. Presley.

TYLER COUNTY,TEXAS MARRIAGE RECORDS 1847-1888. $8.95. Ingmire.

UPSHUR

Created and organized 1846 from Harrison and Nacogdoches Counties, named for U.S. Secretary of State Abel P. Upshur. County seat Gilmer; other towns include Bettie, Diana and Big Sandy. Bounded by Wood, Camp, Morris, Marion, Harrison, Gregg and Smith Counties.

UPSHUR COUNTY CENSUS RECORDS 1850. Index. $16.00.Heritage

TEXAS CENSUS 1850. Vol. 19. Compiled by V.K. Carpenter.1979. Reprint ed., pc. $10.00. Presley.

UPTON

Created 1867 from Tom Green County, organized 1910, named for brothers John C. and William F. Upton. County seat Rankin; other towns include McCamey, McElroy and Midkiff. Bounded by Ector, Midland, Glasscock, Reagan, Crockett and Crane Counties.

INVENTORY OF COUNTY RECORDS UPTON COUNTY COURTHOUSE RANKIN, TEXAS. Compiled by R.M. Olien,et al. Denton,Tx. 1977. 165p. map, index, 4to, pc. $1.00. TSL.

UVALDE

Created 1850 from Bexar County, organized 1856, named for Mexican Indian fighter Captain Juan de Ugalde. County seat Uvalde; other towns include Utopia, Sabinal and Knippa. Bounded by Edwards, Real, Frio, Bandera, Medina, Zavala, Maverick and Kinney Counties.

UVALDE HERITAGE HOMES. By Jane Knapik. Uvalde,Tx. 1982. $9.50. Knapik.

VAL VERDE

Created and organized 1885 from Crockett, Kinney and Pecos Counties, named for Civil War Battle of Val Verde in New Mexico. County seat Del Rio; other towns include Comstock and Langtry. Bounded by Terrell, Crockett, Sutton, Edwards and Kinney Counties, and by Mexico on the south.

A HISTORY OF SAN FELIPE. Compiled by A.E. Gutierrez. Del Rio,Tx.,1978. 32p.,ill., 4to, pc. $3.00. Whitehead.

VAN ZANDT

Created and organized 1848 from Henderson County, named for early Texas politician Isaac Van Zandt. County seat Canton; other towns include Edgewood, Ben Wheeler, Grand Saline, Van and Wills Point. Bounded by Kaufman, Hunt, Rains, Wood, Smith and Henderson Counties.

EARLY SCHOLASTIC RECORDS OF VAN ZANDT COUNTY,TEXAS 1889-1901. Compiled by Mrs. E. Valandingham and Mrs. Exa Thomas pc. $5.00. Thomas.

EVERY FIRST MONDAY. A History of Canton,Texas. By David N. Wren. Quanah, 1973. 91p.,ill. $8.00. Ranger.

A HISTORY OF VAN ZANDT COUNTY. By M.E. Hall. Austin, 1976. 156p., $12.50. Ranger.

INVENTORY OF RECORDS VAN ZANDT COUNTY COURTHOUSE CANTON, TEXAS. Compiled by Margaret E. Hall. Denton,Tx. 1978. 215p.,map, index. 4to, pc. $1.00. TSL.

MARTIN'S MILL. By C.M. Wallace. Quanah, 1976. 136p.,ill., $8.00. Ranger.

SOME HISTORY OF VAN ZANDT COUNTY. By Wentworth Manning. Wills Point,Tx. 1919. 1982 reprint ed. $18.00. Laney.

"THE SOUTHLAND". Reproduction of periodical containing material on Van Zandt County. 26p. + 7p. index. pc. $3.50. Sanders.

VAN ZANDT COUNTY CENSUS RECORDS 1850. Index. $8.00. Heritage.

VAN ZANDT COUNTY CENSUS 1850. pc. $4.00. Van.

TEXAS CENSUS 1850. Vol. 16. Compiled by V.K. Carpenter. 1979. Reprint ed. pc. $10.00. Presley.

VAN ZANDT COUNTY CENSUS 1860. pc. $8.75. Van.

VAN ZANDT COUNTY CENSUS 1880. pc. $9.95. Van.

VAN ZANDT COUNTY, TEXAS MARRIAGE RECORDS 1855-1880. Compiled by F.T. Ingmire. St. Louis,Mo. 1979. 49p.,index,4to. pc. $10.95. Ingmire.

VAN ZANDT COUNTY MARRIAGES. 1855-1884. pc. $8.00. Van.

VAN ZANDT COUNTY MARRIAGES 1884-1888. pc. $3.75. Van.

VAN ZANDT COUNTY SCHOLASTIC RECORDS 1890-91. pc. $6.75. Van.

Periodical: OUR HERITAGE. Quarterly of the Genealogical Society of Van Zandt County. $10 per year. Van.

VICTORIA

Created 1836 from Municipality of Victoria, organized 1837, named for the original settlement Nuestra Senora de Guadalupe de Jesus Victoria. County seat Victoria; other towns include McFaddin, Placedo, Nursery, Bloomington and Inez. Bounded by Goliad, DeWitt, Lavaca, Jackson, Calhoun and Refugio Counties.

THE EMPRESARIO, DON MARTIN DELEON. By A.B.J. Hammett. 1971. $15.00. Plaza.

REFLECTIONS OF OLD VICTORIA. By Robert W. Shook and James Fitzhenry. 1979. $25.00. Plaza.

A 300 YEAR SAMPLER. By Tom Jones. 1974. pc. $15.00.Plaza.

VICTORIA COUNTY CENSUS RECORDS 1850. Index. $9.50.Heritage.

TEXAS CENSUS 1850. Vol. 2. Compiled by V.K. Carpenter. 1979. Reprint ed. pc. $10.00. Presley.

VICTORIA COUNTY,TEXAS MARRIAGE RECORDS 1838-1890. Compiled by F.T. Ingmire. $8.95. Ingmire.

THE VICTORIA SEQUICENTENNIAL "SCRAPBOOK" 1824 - 1974. By Henry Hauschild,et al. Victoria,Tx.,1974. 95p.,ill.,4to.pc. $6.95. Plaza.

Publication: VICTORIA-CROSSROADS OF SOUTH TEXAS. Quarterly of the Victoria County Genealogical Society. $10 per year. Victoria.

WALKER

Created and organized from Montgomery County in 1846, named first for Robert J. Walker but changed in 1863 to Samuel H. Walker because the first was a Unionist. County seat Huntsville; other towns include New Waverly, Phelps and Riverside. Bounded by Madison, Houston, Trinity, San Jacinto, Montgomery and Grimes Counties.

WALKER COUNTY CENSUS RECORDS 1850. Index. $15.50. Heritage.

TEXAS CENSUS 1850. Vol. 10. Compiled by V.K. Carpenter. 1979. Reprint ed. pc. $10.00. Presley.

WALKER COUNTY,TEXAS 1860 CENSUS. Compiled by A. Greathouse. 86p.,index, pc. $10.95. Ericson.

WALLER

Created and organized 1873 from Austin and Grimes Counties, named for Republic of Texas leader Edwin Waller. County seat Hempstead; other towns include Prairie View, Brookshire, Monaville, Waller and Katy. Bounded by Austin, Washington, Grimes, Montgomery, Harris and Fort Bend Counties.

COTTON GINS OF WALLER COUNTY,TEXAS 1825-1976. Compiled by M.W. Abshier,et al. Hockley,Tx. 1981. 90p.,ill.,index,pc. Write. Waller.

A DIRECTORY OF CEMETERIES OF WALLER COUNTY. Hockley, Tx., 1976. 176p., pc. $6.50. Waller.

SURNAME INDEX TO THE WALLER COUNTY DIRECTORY OF CEMETERIES. Tomball,Tx. 1979. 14p.,pc. $3.50. Waller.

A DIRECTORY OF HISTORICAL MARKERS IN WALLER COUNTY, TEXAS. Compiled by A.L. Campbell. Hempstead,Tx. 1977. 25p.,maps, 4to. pc. $1.00. Waller.

FORMER POST OFFICES OF WALLER COUNTY. Compiled by M.W. Abshier, et al. Hockley,Tx. 1977. 69p.,index. pc. $5.00.Waller.

A HISTORY OF THE AREA SERVED BY TRI-COUNTY CIVIC CLUB. By M. Abshier. ca. 1978. 19p., 4to.,pc. Write. Waller.

A HISTORY OF WALLER COUNTY,TEXAS. By George R. Woolfolk, et al. Waco, 1973. 719p.,ill.,index. $10.00. Waller.

WARD

Created 1887 from Tom Green County, organized 1892, named for Texas Republic soldier-politician Thomas W. Ward. County seat Monahans; other towns include Barstow and Pyote. Bounded by Pecos, Reeves, Loving, Winkler, Ector and Crane Counties.

WARD COUNTY, TEXAS MARRIAGE RECORDS 1893-1945. Compiled by C.E. Ericson and F.T. Ingmire. index, $10.95. Ingmire.

WASHINGTON

Created 1836, organized 1837, named for George Washington. County seat Brenham; other towns include Burton, Independence, Chappell Hill and William Penn. Bounded by Fayette, Lee, Burleson, Brazos, Grimes, Waller and Austin Counties.

AUSTIN COLONY PIONEERS. Including History of Bastrop,Fayette, Grimes, Montgomery and Washington Counties. By Worth S. Ray. Austin, 1970. Reprint of 1949 ed. 378p., ill.,index. $17.50. Ranger.

BAYLOR AT INDEPENDENCE. By Lois S. Murray. Waco,Tx. 450p. $6.00. Baylor.

THE BLAZING STORY OF WASHINGTON COUNTY. By W.O. Dietrick. Quanah,Tx. 1973. Revised ed. 190p.,ill.,biblio.$11.00.Ranger.

THE HISTORY OF BRENHAM AND WASHINGTON COUNTY. By Mrs. R.E. Pennington. Reprint of 1915 ed. 123p.,ill. pc. $8.50.Ranger.

INVENTORY OF COUNTY RECORDS WASHINGTON COUNTY COURTHOUSE BRENHAM, TEXAS. 1977. 159p.,map,index, 4to. pc. $1.00. TSL.

WASHINGTON COUNTY CENSUS RECORDS 1850. Index. $19.00. Heritage.

TEXAS CENSUS 1850. Vol. 6. Compiled by V.K. Carpenter. 1979. Reprint ed. pc. $10.00. Presley.

WASHINGTON COUNTY, TEXAS MARRIAGE RECORDS 1837-1870. Compiled by F.T. Ingmire. St.Louis, 1980. 57p.,index,4to. $10.95.Ingmire.

WEBB

Created and organized 1848 from Bexar County, named for Republic of Texas politician James Webb. County seat Laredo; other towns include Bruni, Mirando City and Oilton. Bounded by Maverick, Dimmit, LaSalle, McMullen, Duval, Jim Hogg and Zapata Counties.

TEXAS CENSUS 1850. Vol. 1. Compiled by V.K. Carpenter. 1979. Reprint ed. pc. $10.00. Presley.

LAREDO 1775-1920. An Overview. By Stanley Green. Laredo, 1981. 20p.,ill.,pc. $2.00. Nuevo.

LAREDO. Border Boomtown. By Keith Elliott. Austin,Tx. 1970. Offset reprint from Texas Parade Magazine. 13p.,ill.,pc. $5.00. Ranger.

WHARTON

Created and organized 1846 from Jackson and Matagorda Counties, named for Republic of Texas soldier-politician brothers John A. and William H. Wharton. County seat Wharton; other towns include Blessing, El Campo, Hungerford, Newgulf and Glen Flora. Bounded by Jackson, Colorado, Austin, Fort Bend, Brazoria and Matagorda Counties.

WHARTON COUNTY CENSUS RECORDS 1850. Index. $4.50. Heritage.

TEXAS CENSUS 1850. Vol. 5. Compiled by V.K. Carpenter.1979. Reprint ed. pc. $10.00. Presley.

WHEELER

Created 1876 from Bexar and Young Districts, organized 1879, named for Texas jurist Royal T. Wheeler. County seat Wheeler; other towns include Briscoe, Shamrock and Mobeetie. Bounded by Collingsworth, Donley, Gray, Roberts and Hemphill Counties and by Oklahoma on the east.

No Publications Located.

WICHITA

Created 1858 from Cooke Land District, organized 1882, named for Wichita River. County seat Wichita Falls; other towns include Electra, Burkburnett and Kamay. Bounded by Wilbarger, Baylor, Archer and Clay Counties, and by Oklahoma on the north.

BOOMTOWN. A Portrait of Burkburnett. By M.K. Benton. Quanah,Tx. 1972. 65p.,ill,biblio. $8.00. Ranger.

THE HISTORY OF WICHITA FALLS. By Jonnie R. Morgan.Wichita Falls,Tx. 1971. Reprint of 1931 ed. 221p.,ill.,biblio. $12.95.Ranger.

WICHITA COUNTY BEGINNINGS. By Louise Kelly. Burnet,Tx. 1982. 350p.,ill. 4to. $39.95. Ranger.

WICHITA COUNTY TEXAS MARRIAGE RECORDS. Compiled by North Texas Genealogical and Historical Assn. Wichita Falls,Tx. 1966. 21p.,pc. $5.00. TSGS.

WICHITA FALLS IN WATERCOLOR. Second edition. pc. $15.00. Wichita.

WILBARGER

Created 1858 from Bexar District, organized 1881, named for Texas Pioneers Mathias and Josiah Pugh Wilbarger. County seat Vernon; other towns include Fargo and Oklaunion. Bounded by Hardeman, Foard, Knox, Baylor, Archer and Wichita Counties, and by Oklahoma on the north.

EARLY DAY HISTORY OF WILBARGER COUNTY. By C.P. Ross and T.L. Rouse. Vernon,Tx. 1933. 1973 reprint. 216p.,$7.95. Red.

WILLACY

Created and organized 1911 from Cameron and Hidalgo Counties, named for Texas farmer-politician John G. Willacy. County seat Raymondville; other towns include Port Mansfield, Lyford, Sebastian and San Perlita. Bounded by Kenedy, Hidalgo and Cameron Counties, and by the Gulf of Mexico on the east.

PADRE ISLAND NATIONAL SEASHORE. A Guide to the Geology, Natural Environments and History of a Texas Barrier Island. By B.R. Weise and W.A. White. Austin, 1980. 94p.,ill.,biblio.,index, 4to.,pc. $4.00. BEG.

WILLIAMSON

Created and organized 1848 from Milam County, named for Robert McAlpin Williamson. County seat Georgetown; other towns include Round Rock, Taylor, Florence, Jollyville, Leander and Thrall. Bounded by Burnet, Bell, Milam, Lee, Bastrop and Travis Counties.

LAND OF GOOD WATER. A Williamson County,Texas History. By Clara S. Scarbrough. Georgetown,Tx. 1973. 3d Ed. Revised.530p. ill.,biblio.,index. $18.00. Williamson.

A LEGEND COLLECTION. Fact & Fantasy. By Ellen Seals. Cedar Park, Tx. 1981. 124p + 24p index, ill. pc. $7.00. Seals.

WILLIAMSON COUNTY CENSUS RECORDS 1850. Index. $8.50. Heritage.

TEXAS CENSUS 1850. Vol. 9. Compiled by V.K. Carpenter. 1979. Reprint ed. pc. $10.00. Presley.

Publication: CHISHOLM TRAIL. Quarterly of the Williamson County Genealogical Society. $7.00 per year. WCGS.

WILSON

Created and organized 1860 from Bexar and Karnes Counties, named for Texas soldier-minister-politician James C. Wilson. County seat Floresville; other towns include Stockdale, Poth and LaVernia. Bounded by Bexar, Guadalupe, Gonzales, Karnes and Atascosa Counties.

THE COURT HOUSE STORY. By J.T. Jaeggli,Jr. Floresville,Tx 1971. 18p.,ill, pc. $1.00. Wilson.

OUR FAMILY HERITAGE. By A.F. Deuvall and P.A. Rodriguez. San Antonio, 1975. 203p.,ill.,index,pc.$15.00. Deuvall.

WILSON COUNTY CENTENNIAL 1860-1960. Official Centennial Program and History of Wilson County. Floresville,Tx. 1960. 96 unn. pages, ill, 4to.,pc. $1.00. Wilson.

WINKLER

Created 1887 from Tom Green County, organized 1910, named for Confederate Lieutenant Colonel Clinton M. Winkler. County seat Kermit;

Wink only other town. Bounded by Andrews, Ector, Ward and Loving Counties, and by New Mexico on portions of north and east.

No publications located.

WISE

Created and organized 1856 from Cooke County, named for Confederate Brigadier General Henry A. Wise. County seat Decatur; other towns include Alvord, Rhome, Bridgeport and Slidell. Bounded by Montague, Cooke, Denton, Tarrant, Parker and Jack Counties.

EIGHTER FROM DECATUR. Growing Up in North Texas. By Jim T. Barton. 1980. 149p.,ill.,index. $12.95. Ranger.

PIONEER HISTORY OF WISE COUNTY. By Cliff D. Cates. 1975 reprint of 1907 edition. 471p.,ill. $15.00. Ranger.

RHOME. A Pioneer History. By Catherine T. Gonzalez. Burnet, 1979. 384p.,ill.,footnotes, index.$18.50. Ranger.

WISE COUNTY HISTORY. A Link with the Past. By Rosalie Gregg. Quanah,Tx. 1976. 515p.,ill., 4to. $25.00. Ranger.

WOOD

Created and organized 1850 from Van Zandt County, named for George T. Wood, the second governor of Texas. County seat Quitman; other towns include Mineola, Alba, Winnsboro and Hawkins. Bounded by Rains, Hopkins, Franklin, Camp, Upshur, Smith and Van Zandt Counties.

AUTUMN TRAILS HERITAGE. By Steve Ridgell. Winnsboro,Tx. 1981. $8.00. Winnsboro.

HISTORY OF MINEOLA, TEXAS. "Gateway to the Pines". Quanah, Tx. 1973. 138p.,ill.,biblio. $8.00. Ranger.

WOOD COUNTY HISTORY 1850-1900. Compiled by T.Roy Hodson. 1976. 201p.,$23.95. Wood.

YOAKUM

Created from Bexar District 1876, organized 1907, named for attorney-historian-soldier Henderson Yoakum. County seat Plains; other towns include Denver City, Allred and Bronco. Bounded by Cochran, Terry, Hockley and Gaines Counties, and by New Mexico on the west.

THE YOAKUM COUNTY HISTORY. 1907-1957. Plains,Tx. 1957. 24p.,ill., 4to. pc. $10.00. Ranger.

YOUNG

Created and organized 1856 from Bosque and Fannin Counties, reorganized 1874, named for Confederate Colonel William C. Young. County seat Graham; other towns include Newcastle, Olney, Loving and South Bend. Bounded by Throckmorton, Baylor, Archer, Jack, Palo Pinto and Stephens Counties.

FORT BELKNAP FRONTIER SAGA. Indians, Negroes, and Anglo-Americans on the Texas Frontier. By Barbara Ledbetter. Burnet,Tx. 1982. 284p.,ill.,biblio.,index. $16.00. Ranger.

GRAHAM CENTENNIAL HISTORY. Graham,Texas 1872-1972. By Young County Historical Survey Comm. Graham,Tx. 1972. 86p.,ill. 4to.,paper $3.50, cloth $4.50. Graham.

INVENTORY OF COUNTY RECORDS YOUNG COUNTY COURTHOUSE GRAHAM, TEXAS. Compiled by Bill Sumners. Austin,Tx.1975. 99p.,index, 4to, pc. $1.00. TSL.

ZAPATA

Created and organized 1858 from Starr and Webb Counties, named for Mexican army Colonel Antonio Zapata. County seat Zapata; other towns include San Ygnacio and Lopeno. Bounded by Webb, Jim Hogg and Starr Counties, and by Mexico on the south.

FALCON DAM AND THE LOST TOWNS OF ZAPATA. By Patsy J. Byfield. Austin, 1971. 69p.,ill.,biblio.pc. $2.50. Memorial.

ZAVALA

Created 1858 from Maverick and Uvalde Counties, organized 1884, named for Lorenzo de Zavala. County seat Crystal City; other towns include La Pryor and Batesville. Bounded by Maverick, Kinney, Uvalde, Medina, Frio, LaSalle and Dimmit Counties.

LOOKING BACK AT LA PRYOR. Compiled by the Lydra Club. La Pryor,Tx. 1978. 233p.,ill.,pc. $10.00. Parra.

SECTION 2 - STATE AND REGIONAL PUBLICATIONS

BIOGRAPHICAL

BANKS AND BANKERS IN EARLY TEXAS 1835-1875. Compiled by Joe F. Ericson. 200p., index, pc. $15.00. Ingmire. *Contains brief biographical sketches of over 700 early bankers.*

BIOGRAPHICAL DICTIONARY OF THE TEXAN CONVENTIONS AND CONGRESSES 1832-1845. Compiled by E.R. Lindley, et al. Austin, 1941. 197p., biblio.,pc. $15.00. Ranger. *Biographical sketches of the early pioneers of Texas who served in the conventions and nine congresses of the Republic of Texas.*

THE BIOGRAPHICAL SOUVENIR OF THE STATE OF TEXAS. Easley, S.C. 1978. Reprint of the 1889 ed. 950p.,ill.,added index. $42.50. Ranger. *1,740 sketches of early Texas families.*

BOUNTY AND DONATION LAND GRANTS OF TEXAS 1835-1888. Austin, 1967. 908p., $40.00. Ranger. *An alphabetical listing of over 8,000 men who were granted bounty warrants and donation certificates for their participation in the various battles of the Texas Revolution, in the Volunteer Corps and the Army of Texas, with the frontier forces and in the Confederate and Union armies.*

BRIEF BIOGRAPHIES OF BRAVE TEXANS. By J.A.Rickard. Dallas, 1980. 369p., ill.,pc. $8.95. Hendrick. *Recounts the story of the many legendary figures of Texas.*

CITIZENS OF THE REPUBLIC OF TEXAS. 3d Ptg. 586p., index, 4to. $30.00. Morris. *A compilation of 6,326 names.*

COMPILED INDEX TO ELECTED AND APPOINTED OFFICIALS OF THE REPUBLIC OF TEXAS 1835-1846. Austin, 1981. 168p.,pc. $3.00. TSL. *Lists some 3,000 officeholders.*

EARLY TEXAS BIRTH RECORDS 1838-1878. Compiled by Jane Sumner, et al. 1982. Reprint ed. 150p., index. $22.50. Ingmire. *Forty-three Texas counties' records were screened.*

1830 CITIZENS OF TEXAS. Compiled by Gifford White. Burnet, Tx, 1982. 220p., index. $25.00. Ranger. *With information from various sources the author has produced a document as close as possible to a census of Texas contemporary with the decennial U.S. census.*

FIRST LADIES OF TEXAS. A History. By Mary D. Farrell and E. Silverthorne. Belton, Tx. Second ed. 427p., index. $15.00. First. *Biographies of the wives of the Presidents and Governors of Texas.*

FIRST SETTLERS OF THE REPUBLIC OF TEXAS. Two volumes 275p. ea., indexed. Vol. 1. Austin,Bastrop,Bexar,Brazoria,Colorado, Fannin, Fayette, Fort Bend, Galveston, Goliad, Gonzales, Harris, Harrison, Houston, Jackson and Jasper. Vol. 2 Jefferson, Liberty, Matagorda, Milam, Montgomery, Nacogdoches, Red River, Refugio, Robertson, Sabine, San Augustine, Shelby, Victoria and Washington . $19.50 per volume. Ingmire.

HALL OF REMEMBRANCE. The Heroes and Heroines of Texas Education. Dallas, 1954, 56p.,pc.$7.50.Ranger. *Eighty-four selections with brief comments on each.*

HOOD'S TEXAS BRIGADE. A Compendium. Compiled by Harold B. Simpson. Hillsboro,Tx 1977. 614p.,ill., biblio.,index. $12.50.Ranger. *Names and records of over 7,000 men of Hood's Brigade in the Civil War.*

INDEX TO APPLICATIONS FOR TEXAS CONFEDERATE PENSIONS. Compiled by John M. Kinney. Austin,Tx. 1977. Revised ed. 357p., 4to. pc. $4.50. TSL. *65,000 names listed for those approved pensions, rejected and residents of the Confederate Home and the Confederate Woman's Home.*

INDEX TO SPANISH AND MEXICAN LAND GRANTS. Compiled by Virginia Taylor. $9.95. Lone.

JUDGES OF THE REPUBLIC OF TEXAS 1836-1846. Compiled by Joe E. Ericson. $20.00. Ingmire. *Biographical directory of approximately 1500 men who served as judges.*

LANDOWNERS OF SOME TEXAS COUNTIES. Houston,Tx. Vol. 1. Compiled from original Texas County plat maps. $7.95. Ingmire. *Includes Brazoria, Chambers, Fort Bend, Galveston, Hardin, Harris,Houston, Jefferson, Liberty, Montgomery, San Jacinto, Trinity, Walker, Waller and Washington counties.*

LANDOWNERS OF SOME TEXAS COUNTIES. Houston,Tx. Vol. 2 Compiled from original Texas county plat maps. $9.50. Ingmire.*Includes Anderson, Angelina, Austin, Bastrop, Burleson, Cherokee, Hays, Lee, Leon, Madison, Panola, Robertson, Shelby and Williamson counties.*

MARRIAGE RECORDS OF EARLY TEXAS 1824-1846. Compiled by Norma R. Grammer. Ft. Worth,Tx. 2d ptg. index, pc. $10.00. Fort Worth. *Republic of Texas marriage records for the counties of Austin, Bexar, Brazoria, Brazos, Colorado, Fannin, Fayette, Fort Bend, Galveston, Gonzales, Harris, Harrison, Jackson,Jefferson, Lamar, Nacogdoches, Red River, Robertson, Rusk, San Augustine, Travis,Victoria and Washington.*

MEMORIAL AND GENEALOGICAL RECORD OF [EAST] TEXAS. 1982. Reprint of the 1895 ed. 465p., ill.,index.$40.00. Ranger.

MEMORIAL AND GENEALOGICAL RECORD OF SOUTHWEST TEXAS. Easley,S.C. 1978. 661p.,ill., reprint of the 1894 ed. with added index. $40.00. Ranger. *Contains approximately 925 biographical sketches.*

NATURALISTS ON THE FRONTIER. By Samuel W. Geiser. Dallas, 1948. Enlarged ed. 300p.,ill. $6.00. Ranger. *Eleven scientists who lived in or visited Texas between 1820 and 1880.*

PIONEER WOMEN IN TEXAS. By Annie Doom Pickrell. Austin, 1970. Reprint of the 1929 ed. 474p. $15.00. Ranger. *Seventy-seven biographical sketches.*

REPUBLIC OF TEXAS POLL LISTS FOR 1846. Compiled by Marion D. Mullins. Baltimore,Md. 1982. Reprint of 1974 ed. 189p. $17.50. Genealogical. *List of 18,000 taxpayers and county of residence.*

TEXAS CENSUS 1850. Compiled by V.K. Carpenter. 1979. Reprint ed. 19 volumes. pc. $180.00. Presley. *See county listings for volumes available separately.*

INDEX TO THE 1850 CENSUS OF TEXAS. Compiled by V. K. Carpenter. pc. $16.00. Presley.

A TEXAS COLLECTION. Portraits Before 1882. By Margaret W. Rover. Ft. Worth,Tx. 1977. 64p., ill. pc. $7.50. Ranger. *Ancestors of Texans.*

TEXAS FRONTIERSMEN 1839-1860. Compiled by F.T. Ingmire. 104p.,pc. $12.50. Ranger. *List of Minute Men, Militia, Home Guard, Indian fighters. Volunteers listed in alphabetical order; officers indexed.*

TEXAS FURNITURE. The Cabinetmakers and their work. 1840-1880. Compiled by Lonn Taylor & D.B. Warren. Austin,Tx. 1975. 399p.,ill. $60.00. Ranger.

THE TEXAS GOVERNOR. By J. R. Welch. Irving,Tx. 198p., ill., biblio.,index . $13.95. Ranger. *Biographies of all the governors of Texas.*

TEXAS MARRIAGES 1824-1850. Compiled by Swinson. Two vols. Vol. 1 A-L, Vol. 2 M-Z. $12.50. Ingmire. *Lists 8,800 marriages in 59 of the Texas counties. Lists grooms in alphabetical order, brides are indexed, with dates and county.*

TEXAS RANGER INDIAN WAR PENSIONS. Compiled by Robert W. Stephens. Burnet,Tx. 1975. 128p., $7.00. Ranger. *Brief sketches of 435 Texas Rangers of the 19th century.*

TEXAS RANGER SERVICE RECORDS 1847-1900. Six volumes. 790p. total. pc. $60.00 per set. Individual volumes at $12.50 each. Ranger. *Arranged alphabetically with each volume covering a particular part of the alphabet.*

TEXAS RANGER SKETCHES. By Robert W. Stephens. Dallas, 1972. 155p.,ill. $25.00. Ranger. *Brief sketches of 63 Rangers who served between 1874 and 1901.*

TEXAS RANGERS 1830-1846. Compiled by F.T. Ingmire. 171p., pc. $12.50. Ranger. *Over 3,300 Rangers listed. Volunteers listed in alphabetical order; officers indexed.*

TEXAS SCHOLASTIC CENSUS 1854-1855. Compiled by Gifford White. 392p.,index. $20.00. Ingmire. *Lists for 45 counties.*

SUPPLEMENT TEXAS SCHOLASTIC CENSUS 1854-1855. Compiled by Gifford White. $7.00. Ingmire. *Returns for Smith & Tarrant counties.*

THE TEXAS SENATOR. by J.R.Welch. Irving,Tx. 179p.,ill., biblio.,index. $13.95. Ranger. *All Senators of Texas from Sam Houston to John Tower and Lloyd Bentsen.*

THOSE BURIED TEXANS. By Tom Allen. Dallas, 1980. 192p., ill. pc. $6.95. Hendrick. *Burial sites of 2,000 noted and notorious Texans.*

WAR OF 1812 VETERANS IN TEXAS. Compiled by M. Fay. 422p. index, pc. $27.50. Polyanthos. *Veterans who either migrated to Texas after serving in the war, or had some connection with the state.*

YANKEES IN THE REPUBLIC OF TEXAS. Some Notes on their Origin and Impact. By Arthur C. Burnett. Houston, 1952. 63p., pc. $7.00. Fletcher.

GENERAL REFERENCES

ABSTRACTS OF THE LAWS OF TEXAS 1822-1846. Compiled by Rena D. McWilliams. index. pc. $7.50. Ingmire.

ABSTRACTS OF THE LAWS OF TEXAS 1846-1852. Compiled by Rena D. McWilliams. index. pc. $7.50. Ingmire.

AFTER SAN JACINTO. The Texas-Mexican Frontier 1836-1841. By Joseph M. Nance. Austin, 1963. 642p.,ill.,biblio.,index. $35.00. Ranger. *A comprehensive history of the Republic for the five years.*

ATTACK AND COUNTERATTACK. The Texas-Mexican Frontier 1842. By Joseph M. Nance. Austin, 1964. 764p.,ill.,biblio.,index. $35.00. Ranger.

CHECKLIST OF TEXAS IMPRINTS 1846-1860. Ed. by E.W.Winkler. Austin, 1949. 352p.,biblio.,index. $12.50. Ranger. *A listing of over 1,450 imprints. Includes a list of Texas publishers, index of names and subjects.*

CHECKLIST OF TEXAS IMPRINTS 1861-1870. Edited by E.W. Winkler and L.B. Friend. Austin, 1963. 734p., biblio.,index. $12.50 Ranger. *Contains almost 4,000 entries.*

THE COLLEGES OF TEXAS. A Survey of the Lone Star States Institutions of Higher Learning, Past & Present. By J.R. Welch. Irving,Tx. 250p., ill.,biblio.,index. $18.95. Ranger.

CUMULATIVE INDEX OF THE SOUTHWESTERN HISTORICAL QUARTERLY. Three Volumes. Vol. 1 & 2, $12.50 ea., Vol. 3, $20.00. Ranger. *A basic reference for accessing 70 years of the primary Texas history journal.*

ENCYCLOPEDIA OF THE NEW WEST. By John Henry Brown. Easley,S.C. 1978. Reprint of the 1881 ed. 1,100 pages, ill. with added index. $50.00. Ranger. *Early history as well as over 600 family sketches.*

THE HANDBOOK OF TEXAS. Edited by Walter P. Webb. Austin, 1952/1977. Three volumes. $85.00. Ranger. *The basic reference for Texas history.*

INDIAN WARS AND PIONEERS OF TEXAS 1822-1874. By John Henry Brown. Easley,S.C. 1978. Reprint of 1880 ed. 1,082p.,with added full name index. $50.00. Ranger. *History along with sketches of 536 individuals and their families.*

EVERY NAME INDEX TO THE "INDIAN WARS AND PIONEERS OF TEXAS" by John Henry Brown. Compiled by Hunter McClean. 1976. 12p. $2.50. TSGS. *7,000 entries.*

JOURNALS OF THE CONFEDERATE LEGISLATURES OF TEXAS. 1861-1864. Eight volumes. Most are still available. Write. TSL.

1,001 TEXAS PLACE NAMES. By Fred A. Tarpley. Austin, 1980. 256p.,ill. pc. $5.95. cloth $14.95. Ranger.

PAPERS OF THE TEXAS REVOLUTION 1835-1836. Edited by John H. Jenkins. Austin,Tx. Ten volumes, over 5,000pages. 102page index. $145.00. Ranger. *Compilation of orginal source materials with other 4,000 letters from 300 locations.*

POST OFFICE PAPERS OF THE REPUBLIC OF TEXAS. Edited by James M. Day. Austin. Vol. 1, 1836-1839; Vol. 2, 1839-1840. 238 & 239p. $4.50 each volume. TSL. *Each volume records the legislation affecting the Post Office Department, the correspondence received and the ledger accounts.*

THE PUBLIC LANDS OF TEXAS 1519-1970. By Thomas L. Miller. Norman,Ok. 1972. 341p.,ill.,biblio.,index. pc. $10.95, cloth $21.95. Ranger. *An historical survey concerning the development and ownership of Texas public lands with some geographical description and information.*

RANGERS AND PIONEERS OF TEXAS. By A.J. Sowell. N.Y., 1964. Reprint of the 1884 ed. 411p.,ill. $20.00. Ranger.

TEXAS. The Texas Monthly Guidebook. By Patricia Sharpe & Robert S. Weddle. Austin, 1982. 784p.,pc. $12.00. Ranger.

TEXAS ALMANAC and State Industrial Guide. 1982-1983. Dallas, 1981. 640p.,ill.,index, pc. $4.95. TexAl. *One of the best of the Texas guides for 124 years.*

TEXAS CEMETERY INSCRIPTIONS. A Source Index. Compiled by Sherry Crofford-Gould. 1977. 52p., pc. $5.00. LE.

TEXAS GHOSTTOWN ENCYCLOPEDIA. By Ed Bartholomew. Ft. Davis,Tx. 1982. 112p.,pc. $7.95. Bartholomew.*Lists over 1,750 ghost sites in Texas.*

TEXAS IN THE CONFEDERACY. Military Installations, Economy and People. By Bill Windsor. Hillsboro,Tx. 1978. 154p.,ill.,biblio.,index. 4to. $12.50. Ranger. *People,places,events within the confines of Texas during the Civil War.*

TEXAS IN 1776. A Historical Description. By Seymour V. Connor. Austin, 112p., biblio.,index. $15.00. Ranger. *Spanish activities in Texas in the 1770's.*

TEXAS POSTAL HISTORY HANDBOOK. By Charles Deaton. Houston, Tx. 1981. 2d Ptg. 245p.,ill. 4to, pc. $30.00. Deaton.

TEXAS REFERENCE SOURCES. A Selective Guide. Edited by Lois Bebout. Austin, 1978. Revised ed. 164p., index. 4to. pc. $8.00. TLA. *Provides subject access to reference works about Texas.*

THE TEXAS REPUBLIC. A Social and Economic History. Austin, 352p.,pc. $8.95. Ranger. *Fact filled description of life in the Republic of Texas.*

TEXAS SOURCES. By Rita J. Wright,et al. Austin, 1976. 67p. $4.00. BBR. *Sources of information about agriculture, construction, mineral resources, population and tourism.*

VAQUEROS IN BLUE AND GRAY. By Jerry Don Thompson. Austin, 1976. 148p.,ill.,biblio.,index. $9.50. Ranger. *Primarily an account of the Mexican-American in the Civil War, especially along the Rio Grande from Laredo south to Brownsville.*

VISIONS OF GLORY. Texans on the Southwestern Frontier. Norman,Ok. 1970. 217p.,biblio.,index. $10.95. Ranger. *A history of Texas in a series of narratives on certain episodes.*

INDUSTRY

CATTLE BRANDS OF TEXAS. Dallas, 1956. 34 unnumbered pages, ill., pc. $7.50. Ranger. *Briefly describes 138 Texas brands.*

EARLY TEXAS OIL. A Photographic History. By Walter Rundell,Jr. College Station,Tx. 1977. 260p., ill. 4to. $27.95. Ranger.

HISTORIC LEGENDS OF WESTERN OIL. Vol. 2. Permian Basin and West Texas. By Fred S. Cook. Amarillo,Tx. n.d. ca. 1978. 64p., ill.,4to, pc. $4.00. Ranger. *Vol. 1 concerns California.*

HISTORIC LEGENDS OF WESTERN OIL. Vol. 3. The Panhandle and Western Kansas. Amarillo,Tx., nd. ca. 1978. 64p.,ill. 4to.,pc. $4.00. Ranger.

HISTORIC LEGENDS OF WESTERN OIL. Vol. 4. Southwestern Texas. Aransas Pass,Tx.,n.d. ca. 1978. 64p.,ill., 4to. pc. $4.00. Ranger.

OIL IN WEST TEXAS AND NEW MEXICO. A Pictorial History of the Permian Basin. By Walter Rundell,Jr. College Station,Tx. 1982. 208p.,ill.,map, biblio.,index. $24.50. Ranger.

TEXAS RAILROADS. A Record of Construction and Abandonment. By Charles P. Zlatkovich. Austin, 1981. 100p.,ill. $10.00. Ranger. *Includes maps of rail networks 1860-1980.*

LANDMARKS

BACKROADS OF TEXAS. By W.E. Syers. Houston, 1979. 176p. ill.,index. $6.95. Gulf.

THE CAPITOLS OF TEXAS. A Visual History. By Sara Clark. Austin, 1975. 114p., ill. $15.00 Ranger.

EARLY TEXAS HOMES. By D.K. Bracken and M. Redway. Dallas, 1956. 1982 ptg. 200p.,ill. $15.00. Ranger.

EYES OF TEXAS TRAVEL GUIDES. By Ray Miller. Five Volumes. Panhandle/Plains Ed., Dallas/East Texas Ed., Ft.Worth/Brazos Valley Ed., Houston/Gulf Coast Ed., Hill Country/Permian Basin Ed.pc.$8.95, Cloth $11.95 each edition. Cordovan.

THE GRAND HOMES OF TEXAS. By Ann Richardson and the Editors of Texas Homes Magazine. Austin, 1982. 208p.,ill. 4to.,$35.00. Ranger.

A GUIDE TO HISTORIC TEXAS INNS AND HOTELS. By Ann Ruff. Houston, 1982. 128p., ill.,index, pc. $9.95. Gulf.

HISTORIC CHURCHES OF TEXAS. By Frank Driskill and Noel Grisham. Burnet,Tx. 1980. 336p.,ill.,biblio.,index. $17.00. Ranger.

HISTORIC SITES OF TEXAS. By J.R.Welch. Irving,Tx. 196p., ill.,biblio.,index. $17.95. Ranger.

HISTORIC TEXAS CHURCHES. By Cordelia B. McFall. Ft.Worth. 1971. 135p.,ill. $6.95. Ranger.

HISTORIC TEXAS HOTELS AND COUNTRY INNS. By Linda and Sally Ross. Burnet,Tx. 1982. 230p.,ill. pc. $9.00. Ranger.

OLD TEXAS TRAILS. By J. W. Williams. Burnet,Tx. 1979. 496p. ill.,index. $20.00. Ranger.

RETRACING THE CHISHOLM TRAIL. By Wayne Gard. Austin, 1956. 24p.,ill. pc. $7.50. Ranger.

THE TEXAS COURTHOUSE. By J.R.Welch. Irving,Tx. 342p., ill.,biblio.,index. $16.95. Ranger.

TEXAS HOMES OF THE NINETEENTH CENTURY. By Drury B. Alexander. Dallas, 276p., ill. $30.00. Ranger.

TEXAS LOG BUILDINGS. A Folk Architecture. By Terry G. Jordan. Austin, 1978. 230p.,ill.,biblio.,index. pc. $10.00. Ranger.

TEXAS PUBLIC BUILDINGS OF THE NINETEENTH CENTURY. By Willard B. Robinson. Dallas,Tx. 290p., ill., $30.00. Ranger.

VIEWS IN TEXAS. A Photographic Tour of Texas 1895-96. Austin, 1974. 112p., ill. $15.00. Ranger.

MAPS & ATLASES

ATLAS OF TEXAS. By Stanley A. Arbingast,et al. Austin, 1976. 179p., 4to. Spiral Bound. $25.00. BBR.

CONTOURS OF DISCOVERY. Printed Maps Delineating the Texas and Southwestern Chapters in the Cartographic History of North America, 1513-1930. Austin, 1981. 22 map reproductions in color & black& white, loose in portfolio, 17" x22", with accompanying booklet. $35.00. Ranger.

THE HISTORICAL ATLAS OF TEXAS. by W.C. Pool. Austin,1975. 190p.,ill.,biblio. $17.50. Ranger.

TEXAS IN MAPS. An Illus. Bibliocartography with Introductory text by J.P. Bryan and W.K. Hanak. Austin, 1961. 40p.,ill. pc. $6.00. Ranger.

RACIAL GROUPS

BLACK TEXANS. A History of Negroes in Texas. By Alwyn Barr. Austin, 259p.,ill.,index. $17.50. Ranger.

THE DANISH TEXANS. By John L. Davis. San Antonio, 122p., ill. pc. $5.95, Cloth $7.95. Institute.

THE FIRST POLISH AMERICANS. Silesian Settlements in Texas. By T. L. Baker. College Station,Tx. 1979. 288p.,ill. $15.00. Ranger.

GERMAN SEED IN TEXAS SOIL. Immigrant Farmers in Nineteenth Century Texas. By T.G. Jordan. Austin, 1966. 251p.,ill. pc. $7.95. Ranger.

THE GERMAN TEXANS. By Glen E. Lich. San Antonio, 240p., ill. pc. $7.95. Cloth $10.95. Institute.

IN SEARCH OF A HOME. The Wends (Sorbs) on the Australian and Texas Frontier. By George R. Nielsen. Birmingham,U.K. 1977. 1982 reprint. 160p.,ill.,index. pc. $10.00. Wend.

THE IRISH TEXANS. By John B. Flannery. San Antonio. 174p. pc. $6.95. Cloth $8.95. Institute.

THE NEGRO IN TEXAS 1874-1900. By Lawrence D. Rice. Baton Rouge. 1971. 309p.,biblio.,index. $10.00. Ranger.

A NEW LAND BECKONED. German Immigration to Texas 1844-1847. By Chester W. & Ethel Geue. 1972.Reprint of 1982. 178p., ill., index. $18.50. Genealogical.

NEW HOMES IN A NEW LAND. German Immigration to Texas 1847-1861. By Ethel H. Geue. 1970. Reprint of 1982. 166p.,ill.,index. $18.50. Genealogical.

TEXAS WENDS. Their First Half Century. By Lillie M. Caldwell. Salado,Tx. 1961. 283p.,ill.,index. $9.50. Wend.

THE TEXIANS AND THE TEXANS. San Antonio. A series of pamphlets of about 30 pages each, illus.,pc. Ethnic groups represented are Afro-American, Anglo-American, Belgian, Chinese, Czech, French, German, Greek, Indian, Italian, Jewish, Mexican, Los Tejanos Mexicanos, Norwegian, Polish, Spanish, Syrian & Lebanese, Swiss. $2.95 each or $53.10 for all 18 pamphlets. Specify to Institute.

THE WENDS OF TEXAS. By Anne Blasig. Brownsville,Tx. 1954. Reprint of 1981. 123p.,ill.,biblio.,index. $8.00. Wend.

REGIONAL

COWMAN'S COUNTRY. Fifty Frontier Ranches in the Texas Panhandle 1876-1887. By Pauline D. & R.L. Robertson. Amarillo,Tx. 1982. 192p.,ill.,index, biblio. 4to. $19.95. Paramount.

PANHANDLE PILGRIMAGE. Illustrated Tales Tracing History in the Texas Panhandle. By Pauline D. & R.L. Robertson. Amarillo,Tx. 1978. 2d Ed. 392p., ill., index, 4to. $19.50. Paramount.

PAPERS CONCERNING ROBERTSON'S COLONY IN TEXAS. Compiled and Edited by Malcolm D. McLean. Vol. 1 The Texas Association 1788-1822. $30.00; Vol. 2 Leftwich's Grant 1823-Sept 1826. $20.00; Vol. 3 The Nashville Colony Oct 1826-Apr 1830. $20.00; Vol.4 Tenoxtitlan, Dream Capital of Texas May-Oct 10, 1830. $20.00; Vol.5 The Upper Colony Oct 11, 1830-March 5, 1831. $25.00. Vol. 6 The Campaigns Against the Tawakoni, Waco, Towash and Comanche Indians March 6-Dec 5, 1831. $25.00; Vol. 7 Those Eleven League Grants Dec 6,1831-Oct 1833. $25.00. Vol. 8 Robertson's Colony Nov 1833-Sept 1834.$25.00;

Vol. 9 Sarahville De Viesca Oct 1834-March 20,1835. $25.00. UT/ARL.

RED ROOSTER COUNTRY, West Texas Stories. By Mike Cox. Hereford,Tx. 1970. 128p.,index.4to. $6.00. Ranger.

TEXAS' LAST FRONTIER. A Brief History of the Lower Rio Grande Valley. By Frank C. Pierce. 1917. Reprint of 1962. pc. $5.25. Hidalgo.

THE TEXAS PANHANDLE FRONTIER. By F.W. Rathjen. Austin, 1973. 298p.,ill.,biblio.,index. $14.95. Ranger.

THE XIT RANCH OF TEXAS and the Early Days of the Llano Estacado. By J. Evetts Haley. Norman,Ok. 258p.,ill.,biblio.,index, pc. $6.95. Ranger.

PERIODICALS

A BULLETIN OF LOCAL HISTORY AND GENEALOGY. A publication of the West Texas Genealogical Society. $7.50 per year. WTGS.

EAST TEXAS HISTORICAL JOURNAL. Quarterly of the East Texas Historical Association. $5 per issue or $8 per year with membership.ETHJ.

THE GREAT LLANO ESTACADO SOUTHWEST HERITAGE. Quarterly. $9.00 per year. GLE

GREAT PLAINS JOURNAL. Annual publication of the Institute of the Great Plains. $6.00 per copy. GPJ

HEART OF TEXAS RECORDS. Quarterly of Central Texas Genealogical Society,Inc. Write. Waco.

MILITARY HISTORY OF TEXAS AND THE SOUTHWEST. Quarterly. $8.50 per volume (4 issues). Military.

NORTHEAST TEXAS GENEALOGICAL SOCIETY QUARTERLY. $10.00 per year. Northeast.

RED RIVER VALLEY HISTORICAL REVIEW. Quarterly of the Red River Valley Historical Association. $12.00 per year with membership. RRVHR.

SOUTHEAST TEXAS HISTORIAN. Annual journal of local and regional history. $1.00 per issue. San Jacinto.

SOUTHWESTERN HISTORICAL QUARTERLY. Quarterly publication of the Texas State Historical Association. $6.00 per issue or $20.00 per year with membership. TSHA.

STIRPES. Quarterly of the Texas State Genealogical Society. $12.00 per year. TSGS.

TEXAS HISTORIAN. Published 5 times per year for the Junior Historians of Texas. $5.00 per year. TSHA.

THE TREESHAKER. Biannual publication of The Permian Basin Genealogical Society,Inc. $7.50 per year. Treeshaker.

THE WESTERN LINK. Publication of the Western Texas Genealogical Association. Write. WTGA.

WEST TEXAS HISTORICAL ASSOCIATION YEARBOOK. Publication of the West Texas Historical Association. $7.50 per issue. Index to Volumes 1-45, $10.00. WTHA.

YELLOWED PAGES. Quarterly of the Southeast Texas Genealogical and Historical Society. $10.00 per year. Southeast.

PANHANDLE PLAINS HISTORICAL REVIEW. Annual of the Panhandle Plains Historical Society. $8.00 per volume. Panhandle.

SECTION 3 - SOURCES

To be used only for ordering specific books in preceding sections.

Abilene
Reporter Publishing Co.
Abilene, Tx 79604

AFW
A.F. Weaver
412 N. Oak
Mineral Wells, Tx 76067

AGS
Austin Genealogical Society
P.O. Box 774
Austin, Tx 78767

Alamo
Alamo Museum
P.O. Box 2599
San Antonio, Tx 78299

Albany
Albany Chamber of Commerce
P.O. Box 185
Albany, Tx 76430

Albany HS
Old Timer, Albany High School
Box 188
Albany, Tx 76430

Alcalde
Alcalde Productions
5310 San Pedro
San Antonio, Tx 78212

Amarillo
Amarillo Genealogical Society
P.O. Box 2171
Amarillo, Tx 79189

Angelo
A. de Leon, Dept. of History
Angelo State University
San Angelo, Tx 76909

Anthony
Helen B. Anthony
P.O. Box 3855
Dallas, Tx 75208

Applen
June Applen
Route 4 Box 482
Quinlan, Tx 75474

APS
Abilene Printing & Stationery Co.
P.O. Box 1560
Abilene, Tx 79604
(915) 677-2673

Archer
Archer County Historical Comm.
Jack Loftin
Route 1
Windthorst, Tx 76389

Athens
Athens Genealogical Organization
c/o Henderson County Library
121 Prairieville St.
Athens, Tx 75751

Austin
Austin-Travis County Collection
Austin Public Library
P.O. Box 2287
Austin, Tx 78768

Barber
Rt. 2 Box 222
Lufkin, Tx 75901

Bartholomew
Ed Bartholomew
P.O. Box 805
Ft. Davis, Tx 79734
(915) 426-3359

Battle
Battle of Fort Anahuac Committee
Drawer D
Anahuac, Tx 77514

Bay
First United Methodist Church
2300 Avenue H
Bay City, Tx 77414

Baylor
Book Department
Baylor Book Store
P.O. Box 6325
Waco, Tx 76706

BBR
Bureau of Business Research
The University of Texas
Austin, Tx 78712
(512) 471-1616

Beeville
Beeville Bee-Picayune
P.O. Box 10
Beeville, Tx 78102

BEG
Bureau of Economic Geology
The University of Texas at Austin
University Station Box X
Austin, Tx 78712
(512) 471-7721

Bell
Bell County Historical Comm.
Berneta Peeples
702 N. Pearl St.
Belton, Tx 76513

Black
Mrs. Erma Black
717 Burnside St.
Rotan, Tx 79546

Bland
Jeanette B. Bland
1426 North Cheyenne
Richardson, Tx 75080

Boerne
The Genealogical Society of
Kendall County, Texas
Box 623
Boerne, Tx 78006

Boring
Frank Boring
Franklin, Tx 77856

Bottom
Odette Bottom
Box 2
Abbott, Tx 76621

Bowden
Mrs. L.B. Bowden
Rt. 1
Dimmitt, Tx 79027

Bowman
Bowman Printing Co.
Rt. 1 Box 183-A
Atlanta, Tx 75551

Brady
Mrs. John G. Jones
705 W. 14th
Brady, Tx 76825

Brasher
Lillian Brasher
226 Sandalwood
Levelland, Tx 79336

Brazoria
Brazoria County Historical Comm.
Beth Griggs
Box 1222
Angleton, Tx 77515

Brazos
The Brazos Genealogical Assn.
Rt. 4 Box 440
College Station, Tx 77840

Brazosport
Brazosport Genealogical Society
P.O. Box 813
Lake Jackson, Tx 77566

BRI
B-RI Railroad Museum
208 S. 3rd Ave.
Teague, Tx 75860

Bridges
C.A. Bridges
Box 2302
Denton, Tx 76201

Briscoe
Briscoe County Historical Comm.
Carrie D. Dickerson
Rt. 1, Box 93
Silverton, Tx 79257

Brownsville
The Brownsville Historical Assn.
Robert B. Vezzetti,President
Box 840
Brownsville,Tx 78520

Bruce
Leona Bruce
Box 335
Santa Anna, Tx 76878

Bullard
Bullard Community Library Assn.
Bullard, Tx 75757

Burleson
Burleson County Historical Soc.
705 West Buck
Caldwell, Tx 77836

Byrd
Jo Ann Byrd
Rt 2 Box 216A
Weatherford, Tx 76086

CAGE
CAGE
220 S. Bonham St.
Cleveland, Tx 77327

Calhoun
Calhoun County Genealogical Soc.
P.O. Box 1150
Port Lavaca, Tx 77979

Calvert
First Baptist Church
Calvert, Tx 77837

Cammac
Cammac Agency
105 W. Pearl
Granbury, Tx 76048

Capps
Joyce Capps
Box 26
Fredonia, Tx 76842

Carson
Carson County Historical Comm.
Box 186
Panhandle, Tx 79068

Cass
Cass County Genealogical Society
P.O. Box 511
Atlanta, Tx 75551

Castro
Castro County Historical Comm.
P.O. Box 911
Dimmitt, Tx 79027

Cathey
Viola Cathey
Rt 4 Box 211
Gatesville, Tx 76528

Cawthon
Juanita D. Cawthon
844 Acklen St.
Shreveport, LA 71104

Cawyer
Shirley Cawyer
P.O. Box 164
Stephenville, Tx 76401

Cayote
Cayote Publishing Co.
Box 45
Tornillo, Tx 79853

CCGS
Collin County Genealogical Soc.
3724 Yosemite
Plano, Tx 75023

Chambers
Chambers County Historical Comm.
Box 97
Anahuac, Tx 77514

Chaparral
Chaparral Genealogical Society
P.O. Box 606
Tomball, Tx 77429

Cherokee
Cherokee County Genealogical Soc.
Box 1332
Jacksonville, Tx 75766

Childress
The Childress Index
Box 1210
Childress, Tx 79201

Citizens
Citizens Bank & Trust
620 Main
Calvert, Tx 77837

Clark
Kendon L. Clark
1028 Maley Road (Cove)
Baytown, Tx 77520

Clay
Jon H. Clay
3811 Rockbluff Drive
Dallas, Tx 75227

CM
C & M Publications
2505 Stratford Dr.
Austin, Tx 78746

Coastal
Coastal Bend Genealogical Soc.
P.O. Box 2711
Corpus Christi, Tx 78403

Cochran
Morton Area Chamber of Commerce
106 S.W. Ist
Morton, Tx 79346
(806) 266-5200

Collin
Collin County Historical Comm.
Mrs. Nancy Rice
Courthouse
McKinney, Tx 75069

Columbus
Columbus Chamber of Commerce
Box 343
Columbus, Tx 78934
(713) 732-5881

Comanche
Comanche Public Library
Box 411
Comanche, Tx 76442
(915) 356-2122

Cordovan
Cordovan Press
P.O. Box 10973
Houston, Tx 77292
(713) 688-8811

Corpus
Friends of the Corpus Christi Musuem
1919 North Water St.
Corpus Christi, Tx 78401

Coryell
Coryell County Museum
P.O. Box 437
Gatesville, Tx 76528

Coursey
Melba Coursey
Box 759
Brownwood, Tx 76801

Crawford
Helen Crawford
c/o Cherokee County Genealogical Society.
P.O. Box 1332
Jacksonville, Tx 75766

Crockett
Crockett County Museum
P.O. Drawer B
Ozona, Tx 76943

Crosby
Crosby County Historical Comm.
Mrs. Marcia Lockwood
Box 579
Lorenzo, Tx 79343

Cushman
Evelyn D. Cushman
4904 Wedgeview Dr.
Hurst, Tx 76053

Cutler
Garland D. Cutler
Rt. 3 Box B-12
Beaumont, Tx 77706

Dallas
Dallas Genealogical Society
P.O. Box 12648
Dallas, Tx 75225

Dallas East
Dallas County East Geneal. Soc.
c/o J.P. Cummings
515 Freeman St.
Mesquite, Tx 75149

Dawson
Dawson County Historical Comm.
Wayne Smith
404 North 21st Pl.
Lamesa, Tx 79331

Deaton
Charles Deaton
7273 Brompton Road
Houston, Tx 77025

Dennis
Bill Dennis
Box 374
Jacksboro, Tx 76056

Denton
Denton County Historical Comm.
Chairman
Box 184
Argyle, Tx 76226

Deuvall
Aurelia F. Deuvall
Rt. 2 Box 184
Floresville, Tx 78114

Diamond
Dorothy R. Diamond-Collier
3616 Nashville
El Paso, Tx 79930

Diocese
Diocese of Brownsville
Chancellery
Box 2279
Brownsville, Tx 78520

DJ
Department of Journalism
University of Texas at Austin
Box 7818, University Station
Austin, Tx 78712

Donning
The Donning Company
5659 Virginia Beach Boulevard
Norfolk, VA 23502

Downing
Charles G. Downing
Box 825
Eagle Pass, Tx 78852

Duncanville
Duncanville Historical Society
227 W. Center
Duncanville, Tx 75116

Durham
Mrs. Mary K. Durham
510 W. Bridge
Granbury, Tx 76048

Duval
Ernesto Gonzalez
Project Coordinator
Duval County Courthouse
San Diego, Tx 78384

East
East Texas Genealogical Society
P.O. Box 6967
Tyler, Tx 75711

EJ
Mrs. Eva Jones
Box 37
San Augustine, Tx 75972

Elgin
Elgin Chamber of Commerce
109 E. 1st St.
Elgin, Tx 78621
(512) 285-4515

Ellis
Ellis County Genealogical Society
P.O. Box 385
Waxahachie, Tx 75165

El Paso
Books, El Paso Library Assn.
501 North Oregon
El Paso, Tx 79901

Ennis
Ennis Chamber of Commerce
P.O. Box 1177
Ennis, Tx 75119
(214) 875-2625

Ericson
Ericson Books
1614 Redbud Street
Nacogdoches, Tx 75961

ETHJ
Editor, East Texas Historical Journal.
Stephen F. Austin University
P.O. Box 6223
Nacogdoches, Tx 75962

Excelsior
Excelsior House
Jefferson, Tx 75657

Fannin
Fannin County Historical Comm.
William F. King M.D.
1002 Cedar St.
Bonham, Tx 75418

FBGS
Fort Bend County Genealogical Society.
P.O. Box 274
Richmond, Tx 77469

First
First Ladies of Texas
P.O. Box 3015
Temple, Texas 76503

First United
First United Methodist Church
205 South Liberty
San Augustine, Tx 75922

Fletcher
Fletcher's Books
Box 65
Salado, Tx 76571
(817) 947-5414

Floyd
The Floyd County Historical Museum.
105 East Missouri
Floydada, Tx 79235

Fort Bend
Fort Bend County Museum Assn.
P.O. Box 251
Richmond, Tx 77469

Fort Concho
Fort Concho Museum
213 East Ave. D
San Angelo, Tx 76901

Fort Worth
Fort Worth Genealogical Society
Box 9767
Fort Worth, Tx 76107

Forum
Houston Genealogical Forum
7130 Evans St.
Houston, Tx 77061

Fredericksburg
Fredericksburg Pub. Co.,Inc.
P.O. Box 473
Fredericksburg, Tx 78624
(512) 997-2156

Freestone
Mrs. C.E. Childs,Jr., Curator
Freestone County Hist. Museum
Fairfield, Tx 75840

Freier
Paul Freier
Rt. 1, Box 96
Port Lavaca, Tx 77979

Frio
Frio Public Library
222 S. Oak
Pearsall, Tx 78061
(512) 334-2496

Frizzell
W.S. Frizzell, County Judge
P.O. Box 165
Stratford, Tx 79084

FWGS
Fort Worth Genealogical Society
P.O. Box 9767
Fort Worth, Tx 76107

Gatesville
CCGS Quarterly
Gatesville Public Library
811 Main St.
Gatesville, Tx 76528

GCGS
Grayson County Genealogical Soc.
421 North Travis
Sherman, Tx 75090

Genealogical
Genealogical Publishing Co.,Inc.
111 Water St.
Baltimore, MD 21202
(301) 837-8271

Gillespie
Clifford J. Harle, Treasurer
Gillespie County Historical Soc.
P.O. Box 765
Fredericksburg, Tx 78624
(512) 997-8533

Gladewater
Gladewater Chamber of Commerce
P.O. 1409
Gladewater, Tx 75647
(214) 845-2626

GLE
Editor, Great Llano Estacado
Southwest Heritage
College of the Southwest
Lovington Highway
Hobbs, NM 88240

Goliad
Goliad County Historical Comm.
P.O. Box 606
Goliad, Tx 77963

Gonzales
South Texas Genealogical Society
P.O. Box 40
Gonzales, Tx 78629

Gonzales Museum
Gonzales Museum
Memorial Building
Gonzales, Tx 78629
(512) 672-6350

GPJ
Museum of the Great Plains
P.O. Box 68
Lawton, OK 73502

Graham
Graham Chamber of Commerce
P.O. Box 299
Graham, Tx 76046
(817) 549-3355

Grayson
Grayson County Frontier Village
4200 Ansley Lane
Denison, Tx 75020

Green
Green's Creek Press
Rt. 5 Box 174A
Dublin, Tx 76446

Gregory
Peggy H. Gregory
7130 Evans St.
Houston, Tx 77061

Grimes
Grimes County Library
110 Brewer St.
Navasota, Tx 77868
(713) 825-6744

Grosvenor
Charles Grosvenor
5044 Cahuenga Blvd #10
North Hollywood, CA 91601

Groveton
Groveton Ex-Students Assn.
P.O. Box 70
Groveton, Tx 75845

Guadalupe
Guadalupe County Historical Comm.
Joe L. Bruns
404 North Camp
Seguin, Tx 78155

Gulf
Gulf Publishing Co., Book Division
P.O. Box 2608
Houston, Tx 77001
(713) 529-4301

Hale
Hale County Historical Commission
P.O. Box 1282
Plainview, Tx 79072

Harris
Sallie Harris
Wheeler, Tx 79096

Harrison
Harrison County Historical Museum
Marshall, Tx 75670

HCGS
Hill Country Genealogical Soc.
c/o Evelyn Wade
Prairie Mt. Rt.
Llano, Tx 78643

HCHC
Howard County Historical Comm.
Box 808
Big Spring, Tx 79720

Hemphill
Hemphill County Historical & Genealogical Society
Canadian, Tx 79014

Henderson
Henderson County Historical Commission
P.O. Box 1412
Athens, Texas 75751

Hendrick
Hendrick-Long Pub. Co.
P.O. Box 12311
Dallas, Tx 75225

Hereford
Deaf Smith County Historical Commission
Mr. A.J. Schroeder, Chmn
603 Union
Hereford, Tx 79045

Heritage
Heritage Americana
12051 South 1700 West
Riverton, Utah 84065

Hidalgo
Hidalgo County Historical Museum
121 E. McIntyre
Edinburg, Tx 78539

Highland
The Highland Press
Rt. 3 Box 3125
Boerne, Tx 78006
(512) 249-2105

Hill
Hill County Historical Comm.
Mrs. W.T. Smith, Treasurer
Box 72
Brandon, Tx 76628

Historic
Historic Waco Foundation
407 Columbus Ave.
Waco, Tx 76701
(817) 753-5166

Hopkins
Hopkins County Historical Soc.
Mrs. W.R. Tuck
103 Gilmer St.
Sulphur Springs, Tx 75482

Houston
Houston County Historical Comm.
Eliza Bishop
629 North Fourth St.
Crockett, Tx 75835

HR
Archivist
Houston Metropolitan Research Center
500 McKinney St.
Houston, Tx 77002

Hudson
Weldon Hudson
2807 Cedar Park Blvd.
Ft. Worth, Tx 76118

Humphries
James Humphries
P.O. Box 231
Bay City, Tx 77414

Hunter
Hunter Books
P.O. Box 304
Santa Anna, Tx 76878

Hurta
Mrs. A.W. Hurta
Sec., Hawley Cemetery
Midfield, Tx 77458

Hutchinson
Hutchinson County Museum
Box 325
Borger, Tx 79007

Huttash
Ogreta W. Huttash
1502 South Jackson
Jacksonville, Tx 75766

Hyatt
Marjorie Hyatt
P.O. Box 37
Smiley, Tx 78159

Ide House
Ide House Publishers
4631 Harvey Drive
Mesquite, Tx 75150

Ingmire
Ingmire Publications
10166 Clairmont Drive
St. Louis, MO 63136
(314) 869-6596

Institute
Institute of Texan Cultures at
San Antonio
P.O. Box 1226
San Antonio, Tx 78294
(512) 226-7651

Irion
Irion County Historical Comm.
Mrs. Lorena Wilson
Box 547
Mertzon, Tx 76941

Jacksboro
Jacksboro Chamber of Commerce
P.O. Box 606
Jacksboro, Tx 76056
(817) 567-2602

Jasper
Jasper Public Library
156 W. Milam
Jasper, Tx 75951

Jefferson
Jefferson Chamber of Commerce
116 W. Austin
Jefferson, Tx 75657
(214) 665-2672

Johnson
Johnson's Book Store
2456 Calder
Beaumont, Tx 77702

Jones
Jones County Historical Comm.
Mrs. Sylvia Moreland
701 Avenue Q
Anson, Tx 79501

Joshua
The Joshua Historical Society
P.O. Box 256
Joshua, Tx 76058

Junction
Kimble County Hist. Survey Comm.
City Hall
102 N. 5th St.
Junction, Tx 76849

Karnes
Karnes City Chamber of Commerce
314 E. Calvert St.
Karnes City, Tx 78118
(512) 780-3112

Kaufman
Kaufman County Library
106 West Grove
Kaufman, Tx 75142

Kendrick
Kendrick Memorial Library
301 West Tate
Brownfield, Tx 79316

Kerr
Hill Country Preservation Soc. Inc.
Box 107
Kerrville, Tx 78028

Kilgore
Kilgore Chamber of Commerce
P.O. Box 1582
Kilgore, Tx 75662
(214) 984-5022

Kinney
Kinney County Historical Comm.
P.O. Box 187
Brackettville,Tx 78832

Kleberg
County Court House
Ist Office inside west entrance
East Kleberg
Kingsville, Texas 78363

Knapik
Jane Knapik
909 S. Park
Uvalde, Tx 78801

Laake
Mrs. Doris Laake
P.O. Box 109
Paige, Tx 78659

LaGrange
Museum Gift Shop
855 S. Jefferson
LaGrange, Tx 78945

Lamesa
Lamesa Area Genealogical Society
Box 1090
Lamesa, Texas 79331

Lampasas
Lampasas Public Library
P.O. Box 308
Lampasas, Tx 76550
(512) 556-3251

Lane
Mary Lane
5125 Roberta Drive
Ft. Worth, Tx 76118

Laney
Faye Laney
410 W. James
Wills Point, Tx 75169

Lawler
Ruth C. Lawler
P.O. Box 340
Castroville, Tx 78009

LE
Limited Editions
P.O. Box 18673
San Antonio, Tx 78218

Lemming
Mrs. Ruth Lemming
2201 Hayes Road # 3913
Houston, Tx 77077

Leon
Leon County Genealogical Soc.
P.O. Box 500
Centerville, Tx 75833

Leonard
Leonard Centennial Commission
Box 157
Leonard, Tx 75452

Levelland
Levelland Area Chamber of Commerce
1101 Avenue H.
Levelland, Tx 79336
(806) 894-3157

LGHS
Lufkin Genealogical and Historical Society
107 E. Lufkin Ave.
Lufkin, Tx 75901

Liberty
Liberty County Historical Comm.
Sandra Pickett
Box 23
Liberty, Tx 77575

Lipscomb
Lipscomb County Historical Comm.
Mrs. Velma Barton, Chmn
Route 3
Canadian, Tx 79014

Llano
Llano Chamber of Commerce
700 Bessemer
Llano, Tx 78643

Lloyd
Lela Latch Lloyd
1411 Ave. D
Cisco, Tx 76437

Lone
Lone Star Press
2100 Hartford
Austin,Tx 78703

Longview
Longview Chamber of Commerce
P.O. Box 472
Longview, Tx 75606
(214) 757-3333

Love
Love Abstract Co.
Franklin, Tx 77856

LSU
LSU Press
Baton Rouge, La. 70803

LTN
Harris County Genealogical Soc.
P.O. Box 391
Pasadena, Tx 77501

Lufkin
Lufkin Printing Company
Box 589
Lufkin, Tx 75901

Lynn
Frank P. Hill
c/o The Lynn County News
Tahoka, Tx 79373

Lytle
Lytle City Office
c/o Josie Campa
Lytle, Tx 78052

McCarver
Norman L. McCarver,Jr.
Hearne, Tx 77859

McCown
Leonard J. McCown
217 W. 14th St.
Irving, Tx 75060

McCoy
Patricia R. McCoy
706 Shelbyville St.
Center, Tx 75935

McMullen
McMullen County Historical Commission
Box 235
Tilden, Tx 78072

McMurry
McMurry College Books
14th St. at Sayles Blvd.
Abilene, Tx 79601

McWilliams
Rena D. McWilliams
Box 1401
George West, Tx 78022

Madison
Madison County Genealogical Soc.
P.O. Box 26
Madisonville, Tx 77864

Maloney
Vance J. Maloney
506 Hereford St.
Glen Rose, Tx 76043

Mason
Mason County Historical Comm.
Jane Hoerster, Chmn
Box 524
Mason, Tx 76856

Matagorda
Matagorda County Genealogical Society
P.O. Box 264
Bay City, Tx 77414

Memorial
Texas Memorial Museum
2400 Trinity
Austin, Tx 78705

Mesquite
Mesquite Historical and Genealogical Society
P.O. Box 165
Mesquite, Tx 75149

Metro
Metropolitan Lubbock
P.O. Box 1627
Lubbock, Tx 79408

Miami
Roberts County Museum
Box 306
Miami, Tx 79059

Midc
Midland County Historical Soc.
2102 Community Lane
Midland, Tx 79701
(915) 682-2931

Mid-Cities
Mid-Cities Genealogical Soc.
P.O. Box 171
Bedford, Tx 76021

Midland
Midland Genealogical Society
Box 1191
Midland, Tx 79702

Military
Military History Press
P.O. Box 5248
Austin, Tx 78763
(512) 459-9265

Mills
Mills County Museum
Goldthwaite, Tx 76844

Mitchell
Colorado City Area Chamber of Commerce
Box 242
Colorado City, Tx 79512
(915) 728-3403

Montgomery
Montgomery County Genealogical Society, Inc.
P.O. Box 751
Conroe, Tx 77305

Morris
Texas State Genealogical Society
c/o Mrs. Harry Joseph Morris
2515 Sweetbriar Dr.
Dallas, Tx 75228

Morton
Morton Museum Bookstore
Box 150
Gainesville, Tx 76240

Muckleroy
David V. Muckleroy
8222 Gault Lane Apt. 1207
San Antonio, Tx 78209

Mulberry
Mulberry Avenue Books
133 East Mulberry Ave.
San Antonio, Tx 78212

Munday
Munday Chamber of Commerce
P.O. Drawer L
Munday, Tx 76371
(817) 422-4540

Navarro
Navarro County Historical Society
912 West Park Ave.
Corsicana, Tx 75110

NCGS
Navarro County Genealogical Soc.
P.O. Box 821
Corsicana, Tx 75110

Nederland
Nederland Chamber of Commerce
P.O. Box 891
Nederland, Tx 77627
(713) 722-0279

News
The Paris News
38 Lamar Ave.
Paris, Tx 75460

News-Tribune
The News-Tribune
News-Tribune Building
Fort Worth, Tx 76102

Newton
Newton County Historical Comm.
Box 56
Burkeville, Tx 75932

NGS
Nacogdoches Genealogical Society
Box 4634, SFA Sta.
Nacogdoches, Tx 75962

Nocona
Nocona Chamber of Commerce
P.O. Box 27
Nocona, Tx 76255
(817) 825-3526

Normand
Pete Normand
2902 Brothers
College Station, Tx 77840
(713) 693-6526

Northeast
Northeast Texas Genealogy Soc.
P.O. Box 240
Mineola, Tx 75773

Nuevo
Nuevo Santander Museum
Laredo Junior College Campus
West End Washington St.
Laredo, Tx 78040
(512) 722-8351

O'Brien
Dorothy O'Brien
Rt I Box 214
Arthur City, Tx 75411

Ochiltree
Ochiltree County Historical Comm.
Harold Hudson
1705 Eaton
Perryton, Tx 79070

Oldham
Oldham County Historical Comm.
Margaret Walker
Vega, Tx 79092

Orange
Orange County Historical Soc.
P.O. Box 1345
Orange, Tx 77630

O'Rourke
T. J. O'Rourke
1101 Ocean Front Walk #3
Venice, CA 90291

Paducah
Paducah Post
Drawer E
Paducah, Tx 79248

Palestine
Palestine Chamber of Commerce
P.O. Drawer I
Palestine, Tx 75801
(214) 729-6066

Palo Pinto
Palo Pinto County Historical Comm.
Leta Ward, Chmn
Star Route Box 315
Graford, Tx 76045

Pampa
Harris Publishing
Hughes Building
Pampa, Tx 79065

Panhandle
Panhandle Plains Historical Soc.
Box 967, W.T. Sta.
Canyon, Tx 79016

Paramount
Paramount Publishing Co.
1000 West Tenth
Amarillo, Tx 79101
(806) 355-1040

Paris
The Genealogical Society of
Northeast Texas
Paris Junior College
Box 187
Paris, Tx 75460

Parker
Parker County Genealogical Soc.
1214 Charles St.
Weatherford, Tx 76086

Parmer
Parmer County Historical Comm.
Hugh Moseley
Box G
Farwell, Tx 79325

Parra
Mrs. Reed Parra
La Pryor, Tx 78872

Password
El Paso County Historical Society
P.O. Box 28
El Paso, Tx 79940

Peach
Peach Point Plantation Book
P.O. Box 456
Angleton, Tx 77515

Peeler
Peeler's Inc.
219 W. Walker
Breckenridge, Tx 76024

Perry
Perry Enterprises
P.O. Box 200
Boerne, Tx 78006

Phillips
Oma Dee Phillips
Box 615
Lamesa, Tx 79331

Pitts
Mrs. Alice Pitts
1413 Harroun St.
McKinney, Tx 75069

Plaza
Plaza Book Store
117 S. Main
Victoria, Tx 77901

Polk
Polk County Museum
P.O. Box 511
Livingston, Tx 77351

Polyanthos
Polyanthos
P.O. Drawer 51359
New Orleans, LA 70151

Port Arthur
Port Arthur Chamber of Commerce
Fidelity Tower/Suite 300N
4749 Twin City Highway
Port Arthur, Tx 77640
(713) 963-1107

Prairie
Mrs. J.F. Russell, Jr.
Prairie Hill, Tx 76678

Presley
Presley Research
1708 West Center
Searcy, AR 72143

Pyramid
Pyramid Printing & Pub. Co.
P.O. Box 64147
Lubbock, Tx 79464

Rains
Rains County Historical Comm.
Mrs. Joe Weddle, Jr.
Emory, Tx 75440

Ranger
Ranger Press
P.O. Drawer 15247
Northeast Station
Austin, Tx 78761
(512) 926-5876

RCGS
Rusk County Genealogical Society
P.O. Box 1503
Henderson, Tx 75652

Red
Red River Valley Museum
P.O. Box 2004
Vernon, Tx 76384

Richardson
R.N. Richardson Press
Hardin-Simmons University
Abilene, Tx 79601

Roberts
Bill M. Roberts
503 Pershing
Cisco, Tx 76437

Robertson
Sylvia Robertson
515 Archer
Spearman, Tx 79081

Rockport
Rockport Area Chamber of Commerce
P.O. Box 1055
Rockport, Tx 78382
(512) 729-6445

Rockwall
Rockwall County Historical Comm.
County Courthouse
Rockwall, Tx 75087

RRVHR
Red River Valley Historical Assn.
Dept. of Social Science
Southeastern Oklahoma State Univ.
Durant, OK 74701

Rudd
Mrs. Oscar Rudd
1824 W. Ave. B
Muleshoe, Tx 79347

Ruff
Nancy B. Ruff
13 Iris Circle
Longview, Tx 75601

Runnels
Charlsie Poe
207 West Truett
Winters, Tx 79567

Russell
Marie Russell
1307 Pershing
Baytown, Tx 77520

Sabine
Sabine County Historical Comm.
Mrs. Blanche Toole
Box 430
Hemphill, Tx 75948

San
San Antonio Genealogical and
Historical Society
P.O. Box 6383
San Antonio, Tx 78209

San Angelo
San Angelo Genealogical and
Historical Society, Inc.
P.O. Box 3453
San Angelo, Tx 76901

San Antonio
San Antonio Museum Association
Bookshop
3801 Broadway
San Antonio, Tx 78209

Sanders
Mrs. J.B. Sanders
409 Nacogdoches St.
Center, Tx 75935

SanJac
San Jacinto County Historical Comm.
H.S. Faulkner, Chmn
Box 147
Cold Spring, Tx 77331

San Jacinto
San Jacinto College
North Campus
5800 Uvalde
Houston, Tx 77049

Scheffelin
J.J. Scheffelin
2722 Hazel
Texarkana, Tx 75503

Schiess
Shirley Schiess
101 Bluet Lane
San Antonio, Tx 78213

Schleicher
Schleicher County Historical Soc.
Eldorado, Tx 76936

Seals
Mrs. James D. Seals
Box 477
Cedar Park, Tx 78613

Search
Search-N-Print
P.O. Box 777
Farmersville, Tx 75031

Sheffield
Mrs. Ella Lee Sheffield
1215 25th Ave. North
Texas City, Tx 77590

Sherman
Sherman Historical Museum
301 S. Walnut
Sherman, Tx 75090

Shockley
Mrs. H.D. Shockley
710 Limestone
Mart, Tx 76664

Shomburger
Mrs. Paul Shomburger
Rt 1 Box 625
Tyler, Tx 75708

Sipe
Rev. Buddy Sipe
Pastor, First Baptist Church
Cisco, Tx 76437

Smith
Smith County Historical Society
Research Center
409 West Erwin St.,Suite 216
Tyler, Tx 75702

Sophienburg
Sophienburg Memorial Museum
401 W. Coll
New Braunfels, Tx 78130

Southeast
Southeast Texas Genealogical and
Historical Society
c/o Tyrrell Historical Library
P.O. Box 3827
Beaumont, Tx 77704

Staked Plains
Staked Plains Press
Box 779
Canyon, Tx 79015

Stamps
Stamps Commercial Press
102 West Lamar
Jasper, Tx 75951
(713) 384-4271

Sterling
Sterling County Historical Comm.
Dan Glass
Box 880
Sterling City, Tx 76951

Swenson
Swenson Memorial Museum
P.O. Box 350
Breckenridge, Tx 76024

Swisher
Swisher County Historical Comm.
Jack Keim
Route V, Box 10-A
Tulia, Tx 79088

Tech
Texas Tech Press Sales Office
Texas Tech University Library
Lubbock, Tx 79409

Temple
Temple Daily Telegram
Temple, Tx 76501

Terrell
Terrell County Historical Comm.
P.O. Box 7
Sanderson, Tx 79848

TexAl
Texas Almanac
Communications Center
Dallas, Tx 75265

Texarkana
Texarkana Historical Society
and Museum
219 State Line Ave.
Texarkana, Tx 75501

Tharp
Laura A. Tharp
5400 Laurel Lake Dr.
Waco, Tx 76710

Thelma
Mrs. Thelma Bray
1305 Hamilton
Pampa, Tx 79065

Thomas
Exa Thomas
2023 Hillcrest #1087
Mesquite, Tx 75149

Tidwell
Laura Tidwell
Box 203
Carrizo Springs, Tx 78834

Tip
Tip-O'-Texas Genealogical Soc.
Harlingen Public Library
Harlingen, Tx 78550

TLA
Texas Library Association
8989 Westheimer #108
Houston, Tx 77063

TM
TM
c/o G. Spellman
10806 N. Lamar
Austin, Tx 78753

Treeshaker
Permian Basin Genealogical Society
315 West 5th St.
Odessa, Tx 79761

Trinity
Bobby Porter, Cor. Sec.
P.O. Box 386
Trinity, Tx 75862

Troxel
Navena Hembree Troxel
1309 Melrose Drive
Richardson, Tx 75080

Truscott
Mrs. Curtis Casey
Box 675
Truscott, Tx 79260

TSGS
Texas State Genealogical Soc.
2507 Tannehill
Houston, Tx 77008

TSHA
Texas State Historical Assn.
2/306 Sid Richardson Hall
University Station
Austin, Tx 78712
(512) 471-1525

TSL
Texas Archives Division
Texas State Library
P.O. Box 12927
Austin, Tx 78711
(512) 475-2445

TUGS
Texarkana USA Genealogical Soc.
P.O. Box 2323
Texarkana, Tx 75504

Turner
James L. Turner
Bremond, Tx 76629

Twin
Twin Centennial Committee, Inc.
c/o Edna Herald
P.O. Drawer B
Edna, Tx 77957

Tyler
P.O. Box 180
Tyler, Tx 75710

UT/ARL
The UTA Press
Box 929
Arlington, Tx 76019
(817) 273-3391, ext. 72

Van
Genealogical Society of Van Zandt
County
Box 434
Wills Point, Tx 75169

Vantage
Vantage Press, Inc.
516 W. 34th St.
N.Y.,N.Y. 10001
(212) 736-1767

Victoria
Victoria County Genealogical Soc.
302 N. Main St.
Victoria, Tx 77901

Waco
Central Texas Genealogical Soc.
c/o Waco-McLennan County Lib.
1717 Austin Ave.
Waco, Tx 76701

Waller
Waller County Historical Comm.
Mildred W. Abshier
Route 1, Box 728
Hockley, Tx 77447

Wanjura
Mrs. Otis Wanjura
Box 251
Lytle, Tx 78052
(512) 772-4174

Waring
Margaret Waring
Box 753
Comanche, Tx 76442

Washburn
Mrs. Inez Washburn
102 Mesa Dr.
Gatesville, Tx 76528

Waters
Mike Waters - A.L.A.M.O.
402 Artemis
San Antonio, Tx 78218
(512) 654-6687.

WCGS
Williamson County Genealogical Society
P.O. Box 585
Round Rock, Tx 78664

Weaver
Weaver's Drug Store
De Leon, Texas 76444

Weeks
Rev. W.C. Weeks, Pastor
Presbyterian Church
P.O. Box 9
Cisco, Tx 76437

Wend
Texas Wendish Heritage Society
P.O. Box 311
Giddings, Tx 78942

Weslaco
Weslaco Chamber of Commerce
P.O. Box 8488
Weslaco, Tx 78596

Wetzel
Hazel E. Wetzel
3618 Fourth St.
Brownwood, Tx 76801

Whitehead
Whitehead Memorial Museum
1308 S. Main St.
Del Rio, Tx 78840

Wichita
Wichita County Heritage Society
Box 3193
Wichita Falls, Tx 76309

Williamson
Williamson County Sun
Georgetown, Tx 78626

Wilson
Wilson County Historical Commission
Roy L. Swift
Rt 3 Box 51
Floresville, Tx 78761

Winnsboro
Winnsboro Chamber of Commerce
201 W. Broadway
Winnsboro, Tx 75494

Winter
Winter Wheat House
P.O. Drawer G, University Sta.
Austin, Tx 78712
(512) 477-8238

Withers
Mrs. Zona Withers
703 Wichita St.
Lockhart, Tx 78644

Wood
Wood County Historical Comm.
Herman Benthul, Chmn
Box 133
Golden, Tx 75444

Wright
Mrs. Mildred S. Wright
140 Briggs
Beaumont, Tx 77707

WTGA
Western Texas Genealogical Assn.
1916 23rd St.
Snyder, Tx 79549

WTGS
West Texas Genealogical Society
Box 2307
Abilene, Tx 79604

WTHA
West Texas Historical Assn.
Hardin-Simmons University Sta.
Box 152
Abilene, Tx 79688

Wyatt
Tula Townsend Wyatt
1/2 Mile Wimberley Highway
San Marcos, Tx 78666

<u>Yale</u>
Yale University Press
92A Yale Station
New Haven, Conn. 06520
(203) 432-4969

<u>Zachry</u>
Zachry Publications
502 E. N. 16
Abilene, Tx 79601

<u>Zatopek</u>
Mrs. Frank Zatopek
2809 Royal Drive
Kilgore, Tx 75662

<u>Zephyr</u>
Zephyr Community Improvement
Club
P.O. Box 564
Zephyr, Tx 76880

SECTION 4 - OUT-OF-PRINT LOCAL HISTORY

This book includes only a small portion of the Texas town and county histories that have been published over the years. Most of these histories were published in small quantities, even as they are today, and quickly sold out. When the supply of the original publisher or any other immediate source has been exhausted, the book goes into the "out-of-print" category and, if in demand, eventually becomes a scarce or "rare" book. At this point the primary source of the book will be the antiquarian bookseller. But, before turning to the antiquarian bookseller it is necessary to know exactly what is wanted.

To identify everything that has been published about a town or county is not easy. The best single source of information for any particular area is the city or county library. A local history or genealogical organization can also be of help in identifying known source materials.

The best single printed source that lists Texas local histories is John H. Jenkins' **Cracker Barrel Chronicles**, a bibliography of Texas town and county histories. It covers most of the printed materials up through 1964.

After the out-of-print book has been identified, the antiquarian bookseller can be of help in finding it. There are a number of such dealers throughout the state who maintain a stock of books relating to local history. If they do not have the particular book wanted, they can try to locate it from other booksellers throughout the United States.

Most of the booksellers listed below operate only by mail-order; some do maintain bookstores. Contact those in your immediate area or write to the others at the addresses shown.

Alcazar Book Service
Box 12764
El Paso, Tx 79912

The Aldredge Book Store
2909-1A Maple Avenue
Dallas, Tx 75201

Antiquarian Book Mart Annex
3132 Avenue B
San Antonio, Tx 78209

Barber's Bookstore
215 W. 8th St.
Ft. Worth, Tx 76102

L.V. Bolling-Books
3413 Tiger Lane
Corpus Christi, Tx 78415

Colleen's Books
6880-C Telephone Road
Houston, Tx 77061

Frontier America Corporation
Box 3698
Bryan, Tx 77805

David Grossblatt, Bookseller
P.O. Box 30001
Dallas, Tx 75230

Jenkins Co.
Box 2085
Austin, Tx 78768

M.S. Lambeth Booksearch
221 Losoya
San Antonio, Tx 78205

Tom Munnerlyn, Books
P.O. Drawer 15247
Austin, Tx 78761

Albert L. Peters, Bookseller
6220 Dovenshire
Ft. Worth,Tx 76112

Betty Smedley, Rare Books
2509 Harris Boulevard
Austin, Tx 78703

d'Aulaire
Mary Anne Wooten
1122 Colorado
Austin, Tx 78701

Ray S. Walton, Bookseller
1310 W. 42d St.
Austin, Tx 78756

The Wilson Bookshop
3118 Routh St.
Dallas, Tx 75201

Clark Wright, Book Dealer
Mrs. Clark Wright
409 Royal St.
Waxahachie, Tx 75765